Blades, Boards & Scooters

Keltie Thomas

Illustrated by Steve Attoe and Allan Moon

MAPLE
TREE
PRESS

Maple Tree Press Inc.

51 Front Street East, Suite 200, Toronto, Ontario M5E 1B3

"Popular Mechanics for Kids" is a trademark of Hearst Communications, Inc.

Text © 2003 by Keltie Thomas

Illustrations © 2003 by Steve Attoe, and © 2003 by Allan Moon

Distributed in the United States by Firefly Books (U.S.) Inc. 230 Fifth Avenue, Suite 1607, New York, NY 10001

We acknowledge the financial support of the Canada Council for the Arts, the Ontario Arts Council, the Government of Canada through the Book Publishing Industry Development Program (BPIDP), and the Government of Ontario through the Ontario Media Development Corporation's Book Initiative for our publishing activities.

Dedication

To riders and rippers everywhere

Acknowledgments

Many, many thanks to everyone who made this book possible: all the wonderful and amazing people at Maple Tree Press, Kat Mototsune, Word & Image, Steve Attoe, Allan Moon, Mike Simpson, Curbside Cycle & Inline Skate Centre of Toronto, Dwayne McMillan, Stephen Fisher (a Level II instructor of inline skating in Toronto), Robert Chatterton, Sporting Life of Toronto, James Bell, Alex Shear, the Children's Museum of Manhattan, Michael Brooke, Evan Lipstein, the Core Tour, Carolyn Kunkel, Daphne Lewis, Jargon at Know-Ped Knation, Jacques at Old Scooters, and PJ.

Cataloguing in Publication Data

Thomas, Keltie

Blades, boards & scooters / Keltie Thomas ; illustrated by Steve Attoe and Allan Moon.

(A popular mechanics for kids book)

Includes index.

ISBN 1-894379-45-4 (bound).—ISBN 1-894379-46-2 (pbk.)

1. In-line skates. 2. Skateboards. 3. Scooters. I. Attoe, Steve II. Moon, Allan III. Title. IV. Title: Blades, boards and scooters. V. Series: Popular mechanics for kids book.

GV859.73.T45 2003   796.2   C2003-900670-0

Design & art direction: Word & Image Design Studio (www.wordandimagedesign.com)

Illustrations: Steve Attoe: pages 6, 7, 15, 21, 26–27, 29, 30 (upper), 33, 38–39, 40–41, 43, 50, 57, 61; Allan Moon: pages 14, 18–19, 24–25, 30–31, 36, 37, 44–45, 51, 52–53, 54, 55, 58–59

Photo Credits

Cover (main): AFLO FOTO; cover (bottom left): Robert Beck/Icon SMI; cover (bottom middle): Justin Anderson/www.aggressive.com; cover (bottom right): Simon Cudby/Razor USA; 3 (top right): Simon Cudby/Razor USA; 3 (middle left): Justin Anderson/ www.aggressive.com; 3 (bottom right): courtesy Burton Snowboards; 4-5: Justin Anderson/ www.aggressive.com; 7: courtesy of the Bata Shoe Museum; 8 (top right): T. Severin/Bishop Museum ; 8 (second to top): National Museum of Roller Skating, Lincoln, NE; 8 (bottom): National Museum of American History/Smithsonian Institution; 9 (top): collection of the Illinois State Museum; 9 (middle & bottom): Todd Huber/www.skatelab.com; 10 (top): Bill Eppridge/Timepix; 10 (middle): Dennis Nazari/Utah Snowboard Museum at Salty Peaks/www.saltypeaks.com; 10 (bottom): National Museum of Roller Skating, Lincoln, NE; 11 (top): Dennis Nazari/Utah Snowboard Museum at Salty Peaks/ www.saltypeaks.com; 11 (middle): Mark Gallup/Burton Snowboards; 11 (bottom): courtesy Rollerblade®; 12 (top): Tony Donaldson/Icon SMI; 12 (second to top): Simon Cudby/Razor USA; 12 (second to bottom): Bill Bachman/STL/Icon SMI; 12 (bottom): courtesy Time Magazine; 13: Simon Cudby/Razor USA; 15: Deborah Baic; 16 (top): Simon Cudby/Razor USA; 16 (bottom): courtesy Daphne Lewis/ www.dogscooter.com; 20-21: 2003 Douglas Levere; 22: Julie Jacobson/Canadian Press; 23, 28-29, 32: Justin Anderson/ www.aggressive.com; 34 (main): Robert Gill; Papilio/CORBIS/MAGMA; 34 (inset): courtesy Mt. Kilimanjaro Skate Club; 35: Robert Beck/Icon SMI; 37: Todd Huber/www.skatelab.com; 39: Icon Sports Media; 42: Robert Beck/Icon SMI; 43 (top): Zach Podell/Icon SMI; 43 (bottom): courtesy Shaw Millennium Skate Park, Calgary, AB; 46: Icon Sports Media; 47 (middle): Action Images/Icon SMI; 47 (bottom): courtesy Pipe Dragon/www.pipedragon.com; 48: Tony Donaldson/Icon SMI; 49: Bill Bachman/STL/Icon SMI; 55 (left): STL/Icon SMI; 55 (right): courtesy Burton Snowboards; 56 (top): Bill Bachman/STL/Icon SMI; 56 (bottom), 59: Philippe Millereau.DPPI/Icon SMI; 60-61: courtesy MBS Mountainboards/www.mbs.com.

Printed in Hong Kong

A   B   C   D   E   F

Contents

Your Ticket to Rip   4
Get Stoked on Safety   6

A History of Radical Fun   7

Scooter City   13
The Lean Mean Scootin' Machine   14
Zoom In on the Mechanics: The Push 'n' Glide Ride   15
The X-treme Scene: Busting Big Tricks   16
Grease Monkey Zone: Tune Up to Scoot   18
Shear Stuff of Wow   20
That's Radical: Scoot into the Future   22

Blade World   23
The Lean Mean Rolling Machines   24
Zoom In on the Mechanics: Catching Air   26
The X-treme Scene: Skating Aggressive   28
Grease Monkey Zone: Tune Up to Stride 'n' Glide   30
Zoom In on the Mechanics: Going Vertical   32
That's Radical: Skating Up Mount Kilimanjaro   34

Skateboard Wave   35
The Lean Mean Skateboarding Machine   36
Zoom In on the Mechanics: All About Balance   38
Zoom In on the Mechanics: Ollie, Ollie, Up!   40
The X-treme Scene: The Birth of X-treme   42
Grease Monkey Zone: Tune Up to Board   44
Who Rules the Halfpipe?   46
That's Radical: 900 or Else!   48

Snowboard Mode   49
Threads to Shred In   50
The Lean Mean Shredding Machine   52
Zoom In on the Mechanics: The Downhill Shred   54
The X-treme Scene: Shredders Storm the Olympics   56
Grease Monkey Zone: Tune Up to Shred   58
The Ultimate Board Grrl   60

Glossary   62
Index   64

Your Ticket to Rip

They glide, they slide, and they all give you a totally gnarly ride. Whether you want to catch phat air or go huge, scooters, inline skates, skateboards and snowboards are your ticket to rip.

Step in or hop on and get the inside scoop on what makes these mean machines jam and roll. Catch the wave and zoom in on the popular mechanics of boards and blades. Drop in on the X-treme Scene and find out how pro skaters and riders bust sick tricks.

Enter the Grease Monkey Zone for expert tips on how to keep your scooter, inline skates, skateboards and snowboards in tip-top shape. Find out who rules the halfpipe and discover where boards and blades will take you in the future. Fasten your helmet for a ripping ride.

Rules of the Road*

- Always wear your helmet and all your protective pads (see page 6).
- Make sure all your gear is in good working order before you hit the road.
- Put reflective strips on the back of skates and helmet.
- Wear bright clothes, a bright helmet and red blinky lights.
- Know your own level. Don't take stupid chances, trying tough stunts that are way beyond your ability. Keep practicing until you develop the skills to take you where you want to go. Work your way from easy stuff to difficult stuff. And don't be afraid to fall. You may fall several times until you really get something down.
- Always watch where you are going, especially if you're riding or skating unknown terrain.
- Don't ride or skate in traffic.
- Don't skate or ride in sand, gravel or rain. Avoid wet pavement, because water can make your wheels slippery and difficult to control.
- Don't hitch a ride on another skater, rider, car, bus or any other moving vehicle.
- Give the right of way to pedestrians, and follow all traffic and skatepark rules.
- Skate on the right side of trails and paths. Pass on the left side of slower moving traffic. Say something like "Passing on your left" to let them know what you plan to do before you do it.

*See page 51 for "Rules of the Slopes."

A Way Rad Ride

Who invented the expression "rad"? Kids—who else! Kids in California started calling awesome and really cool skateboarding moves "radical," or rad for short.

Get Stoked on Safety

If you think rad riding means reckless stunts and dangerous moves, think again. Rad riders know that safety is the name of the game. Check out the safety gear that no skater, skateboarder or scooterist should ride without. (For "Threads to Shred In," see page 50.)

Helmet
Scrambled brains are no fun! So helmets are made of a hard plastic shell with foam pads inside to absorb impacts and cushion your noggin. Make sure your helmet feels snug, but not tight, and sits level on your head—about two fingers' width above your eyebrows.

Wrist guards
You'll most likely put out a hand to break a fall, so wrist guards are essential for skateboarding and inline skating (but not for scootering, as they can make it hard to grip handlebars). The hard plastic shield protects your palms and extends above your wrist to support against sprains and breaks. As they scrape against the ground, they cut down on the force of impact—but don't clench your fingers, or you'll skin them!

Knee pads
Fall forward and you're likely to slam your knees. So smart skaters, skateboarders and scooterists always wear knee pads. Some pros wear two sets—one over their pants and one underneath. The hard plastic caps spread out and reduce the force of impact. An elastic back or Velcro™ straps hold the pads in place.

Elbow pads
If you don't break a backwards fall with your hands, chances are you'll break it with your elbow. Elbow pads have a hard plastic shell that absorbs impacts. Make sure you adjust the Velcro™ straps to hold your elbow pads snugly.

If You're Going to Fall...

Just fall to it and use these tips to cut down your chances of a serious injury:
- If you're losing your balance, crouch down. Then you won't have as far to fall!
- Try to fall onto your protective pads.
- Don't panic, windmill or flail. Try to relax your body instead of stiffening up.

A HISTORY OF
Radical Fun

Did you know that kids made some of the world's first scooters, skateboards and snowboards to make their own fun? And that surfboards and ice skates are the "granddaddies" of these zoom machines and inline skates? Check out how today's cool wheels and radical boards have evolved.

Around 4000 B.C. *Now That's "Wheel" Progress*

The first wheel rolls into the world in ancient Mesopotamia, a region between two rivers in modern-day Iraq.

Did ancient thrashers rule the road? Chances are no one knows! But wheels like these made chariots roll, around 3000 to 2000 B.C.

Around 1000 B.C. *A Slice of Ice*

Boney blades! If you went skating over 500 years ago, you'd have worn an animal bone skate like this one.

People in the Netherlands, Scandinavia, and Britain strap animal bones or wooden blades on their boots to get around ice in the winter. And tada—ice skates are invented!

Around 1700 *Fool for Spools?*

An unknown inventor in Holland attaches wooden spools to the bottom of his boots to try to skate on dry land in the summer.

1760 *Crashing the Party*

Belgian inventor and musician Joseph Merlin makes the first pair of roller skates and wears them to a masquerade party. But the metal-wheeled skates have no steering or brakes. As Merlin skates through the door, playing the violin, he slams into a crystal mirror—*kaBAM*—and shatters it to bits. *Cra-a-ack!*

Speakin' of Blades & Boards

Gnarly or sick = amazing/ good/bad

Phat = cool, or a lot

Air = getting height between you and the ground

1778 Surfing Hawaii Style

English explorer Captain James Cook goes to Hawaii and can hardly believe his eyes. The locals are swimming out into the ocean on large wooden boards, then standing on the boards, and riding big waves back to shore. But it's nothing out of the ordinary for the Hawaiians—they've been surfing for hundreds of years!

A big board for big waves? Check out one of the first known surfing photographs, taken in Hawaii way back in 1890.

1819 Skates Get Inline

French designer Monsieur Petitbled develops the first pair of inline roller skates. He places three wheels in a line on the bottom of a hardwood plate, which attaches to the foot with leather straps.

Maneuverable they weren't. Skaters tried Monsieur Petitbled's roller skates, and found they could skate only in a straight line!

1823 The Magnifico Volito

English fruit seller Robert John Tyers puts the finishing touches on the first roller skate with five inline wheels and calls it the Volito. The skate has slightly larger wheels in the center, which allow skaters to make right and left turns, and a brake.

The Volito turned things around for inline skates. It's unequal-sized wheels allowed skaters to execute turns by shifting their weight.

Surf Speak

Hang Ten = a trick in which the toes of both feet hang over the edge of the board

Around 1900 Kids Want Their Own Wheels

Bikes aren't very affordable so many kids have roller skates, wagons and scooters instead. Some make their own scooters by nailing a roller skate to a two-by-four board, nailing a milk crate on the board and adding a broomstick on top of the crate for steering handles.

1910   "Bunkering" Is It!

Kids bunker, or slide down hills, by standing on a sled made from wooden slats of a barrel nailed together, and hanging onto to its rope handle for a ripping ride!

Around 1930   Wee Wheeler Steps Up

The United Specialities Company says its new metal Wee Wheeler scooter is a "great muscle developer" for kids and claims the zoom machine can cover "14 to 18 feet (4–5 m) on good pavement with no more than an ordinary step." Even so, kids continue to have a ball on homemade scooters.

A scooter like this one went for $2.10 in 1933—the fancier model with a brake and bell cost $3.79.

1959   Skates Get On Board

Nobody really knows how the skateboard was invented. Some people say a surfer in California nailed roller-skate wheels to a water ski and rode it down a hill just like surfing down a wave. Others say bored kids in the mid-U.S. invented it out of a homemade scooter. Either way, its metal roller-skate wheels made it wobble like all get out. But in 1959, the first manufactured skateboards hit the shelves of a California surf shop, and they were made with clay wheels for a smoother ride.

When clay wheels replaced metal roller-skate wheels (see right) that rattled riders, skateboards got on a roll.

1963   Sidewalk Surfin'

As a surfing craze spreads across North America, skateboarding, or "sidewalk surfing," begins to catch on, especially among surfers. The Makaha skateboard company makes skateboards shaped just like surfboards. Kids at Pier Avenue Junior High in Hermosa, California, hold the world's first skateboard competition. Brad "Squeak" Blank wins with tricks such as high jumps, handstands, and nose and tail wheelies.

Surfers caught concrete waves on this "deluxe" Sidewalk Surfboard made by Nash water ski company.

Fast Fact Kids' push scooters inspired inventors to build the world's first motor scooter around 1900. Maybe that's why the motor scooter hasn't been able to shake its "toy" image.

1963 *Hanging Ten in the Snow*

Eighth grader Tom Sims gets hooked on skateboarding in California. When snow falls at his New Jersey home that December, he can't bear the thought of not skateboarding all winter. So Tom convinces his woodshop teacher to let him build a "skateboard for the snow" out of plywood. He glues carpet and wood strips to the top for grip, calls it a "ski board," and hits the slopes. Soon he becomes known for hanging ten (a trick in which both feet hang over the board) on the hill, and 14 years later he starts Sims Snowboards to make bona fide snowboards.

1965 *Menace to Society?*

LIFE magazine runs an article on "the craze and menace" of skateboards. The fact is, the clay wheels don't grip the ground very well. And if they run over anything, they jolt the rider right off the board. The California Medical Association declares skateboarding "a new medical menace," and several cities ban it. The skateboard fad screeches to a halt as all but a handful of skaters who love the sport give it up.

Did skateboards turn the world upside-down? Pat McGee, national girls' skateboarding champion, did a handstand on wheels for the cover of LIFE magazine, May 14, 1965.

1965 *Snurf's Up, Dude!*

Snowboarding takes off in the garage of surfer and inventor Sherman Poppen. After Sherman sees his daughter Wendy try to stand up on her sled as she's sliding down a hill, he fastens two kid-size skis together and makes a surfboard for the snow. His wife dubs it the Snurfer, combining the words snow and surf. And when Wendy hits the hills with it, all the neighborhood kids want one.

To keep up with demand, Sherman Poppen made a deal with the Brunswick Sporting Goods Company to manufacture the Snurfer. In 10 years, half a million Snurfers flew off store shelves.

1966 *Inline, but Not for Long*

The Chicago Roller Skate Company designs a roller skate with inline wheels to duplicate the maneuverability and speed of an ice skate. But the skates aren't very comfortable or stable and their brake isn't reliable. So the skates roll out of sight and out of mind.

The skate was called the Rollerblade. Even so, few sales were made.

1970 *A Smooth Ride = A Safe Ride*

Skateboarder and engineer Frank Nasworthy comes across some polyurethane roller-skate wheels, attaches them to his skateboard, and goes for a ride. Suddenly, Frank can bomb around corners at high speeds, change direction swiftly, and ride up walls. Frank tweaks the wheels for skateboards and calls them Cadillacs for their smooth ride. Then his buddy Bob Bahne, who makes surfboards, designs a flexible fiberglass board for them. The new wheels and boards make for safer skateboarding, and by 1973 skateboarding is all the rage again.

1974 *A Safe Spot to Skate*

High school students in Ventura, California, have no place to skateboard safely or legally. So the teens collect signatures to petition city council for a place to skateboard. And they get radical results: one of the first skateparks ever built.

1976 *Snow Surfin'*

When surfer Dimitrije Milovich went sliding in the snow on a couple of cafeteria trays in the late '60s, he had such a blast that he set up shop in his garage and started making snowboards based on surfboard designs. In 1976, Dimitrije forms the first snowboard company in the world and calls it the same name as the boards—Winterstick.

Wintersticks came in two styles: the "Round Tail" and the "Swallow Tail" (at left).

1979 *Taking Control*

Even though the Snurfer has a rope that riders hold for control, the snow-shredding machine is known for its uncontrollable ride. Jake Burton Carpenter (see right), founder of Burton Snowboards, describes his very first Snurfer ride—taken when he was just 14—as "pretty suicidal!" Yikes. Maybe that's why he began tinkering with ways to improve the Snurfer's performance and control. Jake added foot bindings, and in 1977 he launched his own snowboard company. In 1979, he entered the National Snurfer Open Competition with one of his souped-up boards and won. Word traveled fast and orders for the new snowboard began rolling in.

1979 *The Hottest New Wheels*

Hockey players Scott and Brennan Olson are dying to skate and train for hockey outside during the summer. One day, at a used sporting goods store, they stumble upon the Chicago Company's 1966 inline roller skates, and think they've found a way. The brothers retool the skates with a lightweight soft boot, polyurethane wheels that grip the pavement and a brake. The skates perform just like ice skates! The brothers call them Rollerblades™, and the skates become the hottest things on wheels throughout the '80s and '90s.

The Lightning™ skate was all the rage in the early '90s.

1987 *It's Now Official*

Just two years earlier, only a handful of ski areas allowed snowboards. But ski slopes "can't keep a good board down." As snowboards get better and better, more and more people take up the sport. In 1987, the National Ski Association recognizes snowboarding as an official sport and ski slopes everywhere open up to shredding.

1995 *X-tremely Cool!*

The first X Games rock the world. Broadcast on TV like a mini-Olympics for extreme sports, they bring skateboarding, aggressive inline skating, mountain biking and bungee jumping into living rooms around the world. In 1997, the winter X Games are added to include sports such as snowboarding.

Skateboarders rock the halfpipe at the summer 2002 X Games.

1998 *A New Way to Scoot*

Gino Tsai, president of J. D. Corporation that makes bicycle parts, challenges his company's development team to come up with a way to get around the huge factory floor that's easier than walking and smaller than a bike. And—lo and behold—they invent the Razor™ scooter, a slick modern version of the 70-year-old toy with a light aluminum frame and neon polyurethane wheels. And it becomes the coolest way to get around.

A rider from the highly skilled traveling entourage, Team Razor™, busts out!

1998 *Shredders Go for Gold*

Snowboarders hit the slopes in Nagano, Japan, to go for gold in the giant slalom and halfpipe as snowboarding becomes an official Olympic sport.

Busting the Giant Slalom, snowboard-style!

Why walk when you can rock 'n' roll on a super scooter?

The 21st Century *Will the Trikke™ Take the World by Storm?*

What makes this cool three-wheeled invention go? "No pushing. No pedaling. Just rock 'n' roll!" says John Simpson, president of Trikke Tech Inc. The Trikke™ may look like a scooter, but riding one feels like inline skating. Riders turn the front wheel back and forth to go forward, and rock the steering column for more forward thrust. All without their feet ever touching the ground! Way rad or just a fad? Only time can tell.

You are now entering...

Scooter City

Hey, you—scoot! Just hop on a scooter and push and glide for a way rad ride. Whether you're looking for your own "set of wheels," to hotfoot it around town or to bust cool tricks, a scooter is your ticket to ride. You can fold it up and carry it wherever you go and then unfold it when you're ready to roll. Today's slick, sleek machines are made of lightweight metal—a far cry from the milk crates, broom handles and roller-skate wheels kids nailed together more than 100 years ago. And they're built to zoom. Check out what puts the scoot in scooters. Discover the force behind the ride, how to grease monkey your machine, and the inside track on the X-treme scene.

Sick Tricks

Get the skinny on some cool tricks that pro scooterists practice for hours.

Backflip = the same stunt that gymnasts do—except on a scooter. Definitely, don't try it at home—or anywhere else!

Drop In = enter a course by riding down a steep incline.

Flying Squirrel a.k.a No Footer Air = when pros jump up with the scooter, pulling up on the handlebars to get big air; then kick both legs off the scooter and spread them out in the air; then quickly put their feet back on the scooter to land.

Wheelie a.k.a. Manual = when pros pull up on the handlebars and lean back to lift the front wheel off the ground.

On your mark, get set, scoot!

The Lean Mean Scootin' Machine

Why hop on a scooter? It's built for speed and you can ride it almost anywhere. Check out how its parts make it one of the hottest rides around!

Handlebars

The handlebars help you steer the scooter. Thick foamy grips cover the handlebars to stop your hands from sliding off their slick metal as you ride.

Steer tube clamp

Need to adjust the height of the handlebars? Just unlock this clamp by pulling out the lever. Move the T-tube up and down or, when you've got the right height, push in the lever to lock the clamp.

Steer tube

As you turn the handlebars to steer the scooter, the steer tube turns the wheels in the same direction as the handlebars.

T-tube

Shaped like a T, this tube holds the handlebars in place. On foldable scooters, it slides down into the steer tube to make the scooter compact for carrying.

Deck

The deck is built low to the ground for balance and control. Some are made of wood and others of aluminum, which is strong and resists denting, but is light—for speed.

Fork

The fork holds the front wheel in place. Some forks have a suspension system to absorb the jolts and make the ride smoother.

Wheel

Some scooter wheels are made of polyurethane like inline skate wheels but designed especially for scooters. Others, like this big wheel, are rubber.

Joint lever

Unlocking the joint lever by pulling it out allows you to fold or unfold the scooter in seconds flat.

Rear wheel guard

On many scooters, the rear wheel guard does double duty. It protects you from splashes and works as a brake. When your foot presses down on it, the guard and wheel rub against each other, stopping the wheel from turning.

Fast Fact

If you're in good physical shape, you can probably walk about 4/5 of a kilometer (half a mile) in 10 minutes. But hop on a scooter and you can ride that far in less than half the time—just three minutes!

The Push 'n' Glide Ride

Whee! Scooters are easy to ride. You just hop on and go! Unlike inline skates, skateboards and snowboards, almost anyone can ride a scooter right away. It's like cruising down easy street!

Foot Power

Push 'n' glide! Your foot power makes your scooter go. It's a simple case of a universal law of motion: for every force there is an equal and opposite reaction. As your foot pushes back along the ground, the scooter pulls forward. And the longer you stride, the farther the scooter goes!

Built for Balance

The closer to the ground you are, the more stable you are (and, if you do lose your balance, you don't have far to fall). On a scooter, your body is closer to the ground than on inline skates or a skateboard. So a scooter is easier to control and balance. And scooters have handlebars that also help you balance. By putting both hands on the handlebars and your stationary foot on the deck with toes pointing forward a few centimeters (inches) back from the handlebars, you are perfectly positioned and balanced.

Feed that Need for Speed

You're scooting along and you want to go faster. The key to gaining speed is timing your pushes. When you push, you transfer energy from your foot to the scooter, so the scooter speeds up and glides. As the scooter glides, it slows down. So if you push during the fastest part of the glide, you add energy that makes the scooter go faster. But if you push during the slower part of the glide, you add energy that brings the scooter back up to a steady speed.

Put on the Brake, Jake!

What if your scooter starts going too fast to control? Brake, for safety's sake. Step down on the rear wheel guard, or use the handbrake some scooters have mounted on the handlebars. When you squeeze the handbrake, it pulls on cables attached to brake pads, which touch the front wheel to stop it from spinning. But if you find that you're falling, step off your scooter. Then, if the handlebars are dragging you down, let go of them. After all, unlike you, your scooter won't feel any pain on a crash landing!

Chiller Thriller

Lee Friedkin had a pressing problem. The fifth-grader wanted to scoot on snow. But the average scooter just wasn't up to the ride—er, slide. So Lee designed a Sno-Scooter—a tool that makes an ordinary land scooter into a scooter that can be used on the snow.

It won an young inventor award in 2001. And it turned out that some sports companies were riding the same brainwave as Lee. Around the same time, they brought out Sno-Scooters (see below)—scooters made especially for snow letting kids galore get their thrills by standing up and sliding down snowy hills.

Busting Big Tricks

A Dog Who Scooters

Woof, woof! Let's scoot! Ruby (left) is a rottweiler who loves to scooter. Three times a week, the keen dog and his owner, Daphne Lewis of Seattle, Washington, go scootering for 7 to 8 km (4–5 miles) straight. Daphne hitches Ruby to their scooter and hops on board—and away they go. Yee-haw! Ruby runs ahead of the scooter, pulling it along behind him. And even though he's not the fastest canine in the west—Ruby balks at trotting faster than about 10 km/h (6 mph)—he's got good "trail

Not long after modern scooters became *the* way to get around, kids began busting cool scooter tricks. Some tweaked the moves they'd mastered in skateboarding, inline skating and BMX biking and invented a whole new x-treme sport.

The Flying Squirrel

Rad scootering took off in 2001. Jaws dropped that January as 20-year-old scooter pro Jarret Reid (at left) rode into the *Guinness Book of World Records* with the first backflip on a scooter. The gutsy rider dropped in on a 5.5 meter (18 ft) quarterpipe and hurled himself high into the air. Then he did a backflip and dropped to the ground for a perfect landing—all on his scooter! Hey, they don't call Jarret the Flying Squirrel for nothing!

Jarret was also busy busting front flips and working on a double backflip. His passion for skateboarding and inline skating drew him to scooters, because they give him a chance to try a whole new bag of tricks. Being a pro rider is "a chance to be the Tony Hawk of scootering," he says.

X-treme Competition

Jarret didn't have to wait long to test his Hawk mettle. That summer, the Razor Rage National Scooter Series burst onto the scene. And kids dug it! Both pro and amateur riders ripped up the competition's street course of ramps, fun boxes and rails.

Each competitor had two timed runs on a course that was anything but a cakewalk. "Are you ready to drop in?" asked the master of ceremonies, over the sound of groovy tunes. If so, the rider sped down a steep launch ramp, and zipped onto the course to pull his or her first trick.

Scooter Tricksters Rule

The riders wowed the crowd with bunny hops up ramps, tailwhips, flying squirrels and, yes, even a backflip. Talk about sick tricks! Twelve-year-old Lisa Grismer won the Sick Trick for girls with a double tailwhip, and Wyatt Reid won for boys with a backflip. But the most rad move was still to come.

Jarret pulled a no-handed backflip on the Big Kicker—the tallest launch ramp in the world. At 10 meters (35 ft), the Big Kicker stood almost twice as high as the quarterpipe Jarret busted the first scooter backflip on. But no worries. Jarret dropped down and got airborne. He let his scooter go, did a backflip, hopped back on his scooter and landed expertly. Now that's a Hawk, er, squirrelly move!

sense," spotting connecting paths and trails and leading the way. He knows to stick to the right side of the trail so faster trail users can pass him on the left. And he learned all by himself how to avoid crashes into other dogs. Once when he found himself on a collision course with another dog and its master, he veered left, passed by them and then returned to the right side of the trail. Scoot on, Ruby!

Sick Tricks

Halfpipe = a U-shaped ramp with vertical walls

Quarterpipe = a halfpipe with just one wall

Tailwhip = jumping up and whipping the scooter deck around beneath airborne feet

X-treme = aggressive trick riding

GREASE MONKEY Zone

Tune Up to Scoot

Not only are scooters easy to ride, but they're easy to keep in tune. Now that's a real boon!

Clean Your Machine

What's the #1 thing you can do to keep your scooter on the roll? Keep it clean! Then dirt, mud and gunk won't have a chance to stick to it and bung things up.

1 It's a good idea to clean your wheels after each time you ride—especially if you ride indoors as well as outdoors. Wipe your wheels with a cloth to prevent dirt and grime from creeping into the bearings. If tar or stubborn grime continues to stick to your wheels, clean it off with citrus cleaner.

2 Wipe down the steer tube, T-tube, deck, forks and other parts with a damp cloth. Scrub away any dirt on the grip tape. And don't forget to clean the bottom of the deck, where gunk can really build up. If your deck is made of wood, check your local skateboard shop for wood cleaners.

3 Clean around your brake—especially between the brake and the deck where dirt can bung up your brake. Then wipe down the underside of your brake where it touches the wheel. (If you have a hand brake, clean dirt off the brake pads and make sure the brake cable is free of kinks.)

4 If your scooter has shock absorbers, which look like coiled springs, wipe them down regularly. Clogs of dirt can seriously cut down their shock-absorbing power.

TOOL BOX

citrus cleaner

CITRUS CLEANER

old cloth or towel

water

2 Allen keys

Different scooter bolts may require different sizes of Allen keys. If your scooter came with an owner's manual, check if it tells you what size to use. And make sure the Allen key is the right size before you use it. Gently insert the key into the bolt—don't try to jam it in—or you may damage the bolt.

Replace Worn Out Wheels

Fold up your scooter and take a good look at your wheels. If they are worn out, deeply gouged, or cracked, replace them with fresh ones. Chances are the bearings inside your wheels are worn out, too. So make sure your new wheels come with bearings.

1 Fold up your scooter. Use two Allen keys to remove the front wheel as shown. Put the bolts aside. Do the same to remove the back wheel.

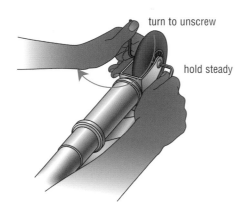

turn to unscrew

hold steady

2 Put the new front wheel in place and thread the bolts through it.

3 Fasten the wheel by using the Allen keys to tighten the bolts. Repeat steps 2 and 3 with the new back wheel.

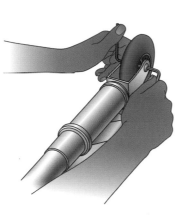

Check It Out

R U ROAD READY?

✔ Check your wheels for wear, cracks and gouges.

✔ With your scooter folded up, hold the wheels at eye level to see if they are worn down more on one side than the other. If so, remove the wheels, and flip them so the right side of each wheel becomes the left.

✔ If the wheels wiggle from side to side, tighten the axle bolts with an Allen key.

✔ Check all the nuts and bolts. If any are loose, tighten them with an Allen key.

✔ Check all the locking mechanisms and have any that are worn or cracked replaced.

✔ Does the steering column rattle? If so, tighten the steering column bolt.

✔ Check the brake. Is it free of dirt and working smoothly? If not, clean it and/or have it repaired.

4 Make sure each wheel spins freely without wiggling from side to side. Loosen or tighten the wheels as needed and make sure they spin at the same rate.

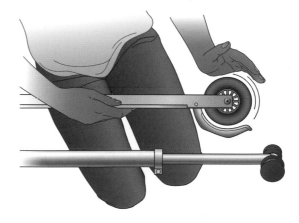

At high speeds, a scooter's rear wheel tends to wear out faster than the front wheel. That's why it's a good idea to regularly switch the wheels from back to front.

Shear Stuff of Wow

Meet Alex Shear and check out some of his "stuff." Alex collects things that make him say the three Ws: Wow! Wacko! Wonderful! He has more than 100,000 objects in his collection. And he says each one has a story to tell—a story about the person who made it, the time it was made and the ingenuity it was made with. Check out some of Alex's scooters, skates and sleds that appeared at the Children's Museum of Manhattan to show what "gives kids the thrill of moving fast."

It Came from Planet Earth...

"I could look at this [scooter] forever," says Alex. The sleek red machine (below), made of metal in the 1960s, looks like it has just zoomed in from outer space. Everything about it is aerodynamic, or shaped to cut down wind drag. "To me, it's an object of art," says Alex. "That's why I love it." It has a beautiful form and a design inspired by aeronautics (the science of air travel). "It looks like it would cut through air and space... When I saw it, it was love at first sight. I had to have it."

What a Gas!

Does Alex look ready to roll, or what? He's all geared up in his gas-powered roller skates (above). He's wearing a backpack motor that drives the rear wheels of the roller skate on his right foot. The whole contraption seems wonderful until Alex asks himself "what do you do with the left foot?" Is it forever playing catch up with the right foot? Well, however the skates were meant to work, they didn't work properly. The company that made them had to recall them. Alex calls this a case of "What were they thinking?" Definitely wacko!

Soda Pop Scooter

Hop on the "Soda Pop"! This wooden scooter is called an "orange skate crate," says Alex. "It's one of my favorites. It's homemade." Someone made it in the 1950s—or so Alex thinks—out of two-by-four plank scraps scrounged from a construction site. Then they spiffed it up by nailing on more than 80 bottle caps, a shiny red reflector and even a seat for a passenger. "It was a speed machine," says Alex, because it had a whole row of roller-skate wheels attached to the bottom, most of which have come off now. So maybe its inventor was trying to feed a need for speed!

Guaranteed to Turn Heads

What would you say about a skateboard with 14 wheels? Wow, wonderful, wacko—or just plain weird? That's what a group of skateboarders, snowboarders, surfers, engineers, and designers invented when they put their heads and testing feet together to "bend the rules of physics." The 14-wheeled board can tilt almost twice as much as an ordinary skateboard. So it lets riders carve deep turns and go with the flow. In fact, the inventors say that riding it feels like surfing without waves or shredding without snow.

Sked-addle

Does this Sked (below) look like it's built to skedaddle through snow? It looks like skis and a sled combined, just like its name, Sked. It's also called the Rocket Ski. That probably means it was built for maximum speed. Very likely, the person who designed this metal snowster in the 1960s was inspired by the space race—the race between the U.S. and Russia to put the first humans on the moon. Wow!

Scoot into the Future

Ever dreamed of riding a scooter through the air? You may be able to one day. Engineers and NASA (National Aeronautics and Space Administration) are trying to develop an air scooter that's powered by two overhead fans like the SoloTrek XFV (Exoskeletor Flying Vehicle). Seen here, the SoloTrek XFV can go more than 125 km/h (80 mph). Besides personal transportation, it may be used as a search and rescue vehicle, flying ambulance, and vehicle for exploring other planets. Talk about a scooter truly out of this world!

The Solar Scooter runs on pollution-free energy from the sun, and can boot it up to 40 km/h (25 mph). It has a solar panel on its deck, a front basket and even an attachment for a fridge. Way cool or what?

Skate straight into...

Blade World

Push, glide. Push, glide! You're on a roll with wheels on your feet. You push forward with your right foot and your left foot glides on the force, or momentum, of the push. Then you push forward with your left and glide with your right...and so on and so on. It all adds up to one ripping ride!

You keep your knees bent, so your legs can absorb the shocks as you dart over cracks and bumps. And you keep your upper body slightly forward, so your skates don't whip out ahead of you, sending you falling back—*splat!*

The world zips by and you might wonder if this is what it feels like to fly. Because when you're inline and on a roll, it feels like there's nowhere you can't go. Check out what makes your blades such awesome zoom machines that run on your own steam.

Can you match up these x-treme skate words with what they mean? (Answers on page 64.)

Words to Skate By

1. road rash	**a.** any move done backwards
2. bunny	**b.** an unbelievably fast skater
3. fakie	**c.** a newbie skater who holds onto things to stay up
4. street	**d.** scrapes and burns from wipeouts
5. sketch	**e.** skating and jumping obstacles in public places
6. blur	**f.** space out and bungle a move

Roll this way...

23

The Lean Mean Rolling Machines

What makes your blades so cool? They put wheels on your feet! Check out how the parts of a recreational blade are designed to help you glide, stop, and roll.

Liner

The liner keeps your foot comfy. It lines the inside of the boot, and sometimes the footbed, with cushy padding. Some liners are made of soft plastic "memory foam" that molds itself to fit the exact shape of your foot. Liners help stabilize your feet, stopping them from rolling inward, so you can control your skates. They also absorb shocks as you skate over bumps and cracks, to help you roll along smoothly.

Closure system

When you're ready to roll, you do up your skates with laces, buckles or a combo of both. Some inline skates also have a strap to give your ankle extra support.

Ankle cuff

This cuff gives your ankle extra support. It also stabilizes your foot so it doesn't roll from side to side. Some cuffs are designed to flex just the way your ankle does when you bend your knees. This helps you keep your knees bent—the basic stance for awesome blading!

Brake

When you want to stop, just step on it, dude! A skate brake brings you to a stop when your heel pushes it down into the ground. It's made of polyurethane plastic or hard rubber that wears out and needs replacing with use.

Boot

Skate designers study the parts of the foot and how they work in order to create the best fit and build for maximum comfort and support in your skate boots. Some boots are made of hard plastic, some are made of soft leather and mesh, and others are made of all three. Since your feet sweat, inline skate boots have vents, or openings, to let air in and sweat out.

Frame

The frame holds the wheels on the bottom of the boot. It's made of aluminum that's reinforced, or strengthened, with carbon. That makes it stiff enough to transmit power from your foot to the wheels without losing much energy, but also flexible enough to absorb shocks.

Wheels

Skate wheels are made of colorful polyurethane and come in many sizes, shapes and degrees of hardness (See "The Wheel Deal" at right). Get the scoop on how your skate wheels work, from the inside out:

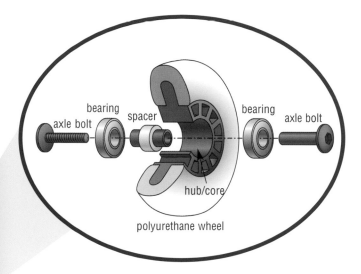

bearing
axle bolt spacer
bearing
axle bolt

hub/core

polyurethane wheel

Inside the metal shield of the **bearings** are tiny balls packed in oil. The tiny balls bear the load of your foot to help the wheels spin smoothly, letting you get the most out of your strides. Here's how. When two things slide over each other, friction slows them down. But if they roll over each other, they make less contact. This greatly reduces the friction, so the wheels spin more smoothly and faster.

The **core** or **hub**, holds the bearings in place.

The **spacer** keeps the bearings from touching one another.

The **axle bolt** holds the wheel.

The Wheel Deal

How fast can your wheels go? And how well can they maneuver? It all depends on their size, shape and hardness:

Size or diameter ranges from 64 mm to 80 mm (2.5–3 in). While smaller wheels give skaters better handling and maneuverability, larger wheels provide more speed.

Shape or profile: wide wheels with flat tops give aggressive skaters a stable base for tricks. On the other hand, narrow wheels give racers more speed, because they have a smaller surface area that touches the ground, reducing the friction that slows skaters down.

Hardness or durometer ranges from 74A to 92A. Soft wheels provide better traction and shock absorption. They also have more zing, or rebound. When soft wheels compress as skaters stride, they bounce back more than hard wheels, returning more energy. However, hard wheels provide a faster ride on smooth surfaces.

GET "WHEEL"

What do skateboard wheels, inline-skate wheels and scooter wheels have in common? Most are made of polyurethane or, as skateboarders call it, urethane. So what makes urethane the "wheel" thing? First, urethane has good "abrasion resistance"—it can roll over rough ground for a long time before it wears out. Second up, urethane grips the ground well, which helps skateboarders control the board, inline skaters control their skates and scooterists control their scooters. Finally, urethane is very resilient. When a skateboarder's weight presses down on a urethane wheel, for example, the wheel flattens a bit. Then it quickly returns to its round shape, without losing much of the energy that speeds the board along. Zoom, zoom!

In 1999, Fabrice Gropaiz of France became the first person to roll all the way around the globe on inline skates. He skated more than 27,000 km (17,000 miles) in 28 months, dodging runaway trucks, deep ravines and rattlesnakes along the way.

Catching Air

Catching air is the basic move of almost all inline skating tricks and stunts. You've probably seen aggressive skaters catch "big air." But chances are they started off jumping small—over a crack in the sidewalk. That way there was nothing to trip them up into a nasty slam. So take a cue from the pros. Put on your helmet and your armor. Then stand in front of a crack and try jumping over it in your skates. Once that feels comfortable, try skating into the jump.

2. Jumping

Lean forward and bend your knees more. Just before you push off, drop your arms behind you for the momentum, or force, to thrust your body into the air. Then throw your arms up and straighten your knees to push off with both feet at once as shown. (If you push off on just one foot, you'll be less stable and won't go as high.) Jump up—not out!

1. Setting Up

Skate toward the sidewalk crack—and don't forget to bend your knees! About 1.5 m (5 ft) before the crack, start gliding toward the takeoff point with your feet together as shown.

Words to Skate By

Air, Catching Air = getting height between you and the ground

Armor = protective pads

Slam = make rough contact with the skating surface

3. Landing

Move your feet into the scissor position as shown. It will give you a longer landing base that's more stable. Land on your front foot first with your weight forward. As soon as your other foot hits the ground, skate forward to stabilize yourself.

So you want to skate aggressive? The trick is to skate smart. Trying to enter the x-treme scene without having the basics down first—forward and backward skating, stopping, turning, crossover turns—is the ultimate bonehead move. X-treme skating is only for pros who have completely mastered all the ins and outs of inline skating. So practice, practice, practice all the basic skating moves to really get them down—and don't forget to have fun on your blades. Then one day you may have the skills you need to learn x-treme moves with an experienced skater or instructor.

Next Steps, er, Jumps

Once you get these moves down, you can try jumping over a small, empty cardboard box, then a bigger box, and so on. But don't try anything that might damage property! To jump higher, build up speed as you skate into the jump. The more speed you have, the higher you can go. And when your feet leave the ground, pull your knees toward your chest for more height. Take it one small step, er, jump at a time!

When you jump, you have to think about getting your whole body over the obstacle—not just your feet.

Skating Aggressive

Y ou're sitting on the edge of your seat and there's not one empty seat left in the skatepark. The crowd is totally pumped. The best pro skaters in the world are at this x-treme event and they're inline and ready to roll!

The Vert Event

The vert skaters are warming up on a huge halfpipe. In competition, the skaters will try to impress the judges by reaching heights high above the ramp and doing tricks on the coping (the rail at the top of the ramp). It takes skill, creativity and radical style to win.

Whoosh! The first skater blasts up the ramp and catches big air—jumping 3 m (10 ft) above the top of the ramp. He grabs one skate and twists and spins like a rocket through the air. Burly! (That's skater speak for "awesome," dude!) Then *whoosh*—he lands on the ramp and barrels back down. The crowd goes crazy, whooping and cheering.

X-treme, or aggressive, skaters are pros who can make difficult and dangerous stunts look easy. But that's because they know how to "style" their moves. Don't be fooled. It takes them hours, days and weeks of practice to master the balance and control x-treme skating takes. And that's not counting all their slams along the way!

Fast Fact

In an x-treme competition at Lausanne, Switzerland, in 1996, part of the street skating course was a police car with grind rails welded onto its roof and hood!

Going for the Grind

How do aggressive skaters grind down handrails? Not on their wheels! They jump onto the handrail and then press down with their skate frame to "lock on" between their center wheels. Or they may lock on with their boot soles or the tops of their skates instead. Then they slide down the rail and jump off. Grinding requires incredible skill and balance, and special skates or equipment to boot. Aggro (aggressive) skates are built low to the ground with small wheels. That keeps aggressive skaters close to the ground for good balance and control. Aggro skates have flat wheels for extra stability and extra space between the two middle wheels for grinds. Some also have special grind plates for extra strength.

The Street Scene

Aggressive street skaters bump (ride down) stairs, catch air off sidewalk curbs and grind their way down handrails. They grind on picnic tables, ride walls and even jump over cars! This aggressive skating style has been developed by city skaters blading anywhere and everywhere their skates will take them.

Some of the best street skating is in skateparks where x-treme street competitions are held. In fact, in 2000 the X Games changed the name of the Street event to Park, because street courses that pros compete on aren't like anything you meet in the street. The ramps, handrails and fun boxes are set up for safety and perfect skating conditions. So the pros can go all out, packing each run with lots of skating tricks like airs and grinds.

FABIOLA RULES

"Go big or go home." That's what pro inline skater Fabiola DaSilva likes to say—and do. When she bladed onto the scene in 1996, she blazed up the halfpipe and pulled 540s and 720s (one-and-a-half and double body spins) while most of the women skating vert back then were still trying to get the basics down. She won the X Games' Women's Vert Competition five times in six years, pumping women's skating to new heights. In 2000, pro skating made the Fabiola Rule, allowing women to compete with men if they place in the top 10 during the qualifying trials. And that's when the x-treme queen broke into the men's vert scene and came in third at the men's trials.

The fab Fabiola learned to skate with the guys back home in Brazil. She was convinced that whatever a guy could do, she could do too. And she just "keeps pushing the limits." That's what makes her fab-io-lous!

Words to Skate By

Grind = slide along a rail or curb on a part of the skates other than the wheels

Vert, Vertical = skating on ramps and pipes to get up into the air

Tune Up to Stride 'n' Glide

What does it take to keep your blades inline and ready to roll? Not a lot. Phew! Clean your wheels and bearings with a cloth every time you finish skating. And rotate or replace your wheels and brake when they wear out.

TOOL BOX

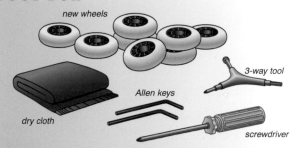

new wheels

3-way tool

Allen keys

dry cloth

screwdriver

A 3-way tool has 3 heads: an Allen Key, screwdriver, and bearing popper. Make an emergency skate repair kit for the road. Just put spare wheels and these tools in a pouch or fanny pack, and away you go!

Rotate the Wheels

If your wheels look lopsided, you've got to rotate to skate! Your skate wheels need to be rotated regularly just like the wheels of a car. The inside wheel edges wear down faster than the outside edges as you push off, turn and stride. And as you push off with your toe or heel, the front or back wheel wears down faster than the center wheels.

(1) Hold your skate firmly as shown top right. Use the Allen keys to unscrew and remove the wheels. Wipe the bearings on each wheel with the cloth.

4 3 2 1

(2) Switch wheel positions exactly as shown. Then flip the wheels—move the inside wheel edge to the outside, and vice versa.

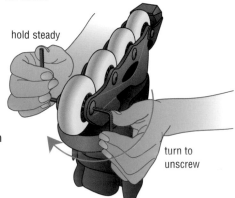

hold steady

turn to unscrew

(3) Screw the wheels back on and tighten them with the Allen keys. Make sure each wheel spins freely. Loosen or tighten the wheels as necessary with the Allen keys and make sure they all spin at the same rate. Repeat steps 1 to 3 on the other skate.

Replace the Brake

Boulder ahead—*whoa*—hit the brake! You count on your brake to stop. That's why you need to replace it before it wears out. Many brakes have a wear-limit line to show you when to replace them.

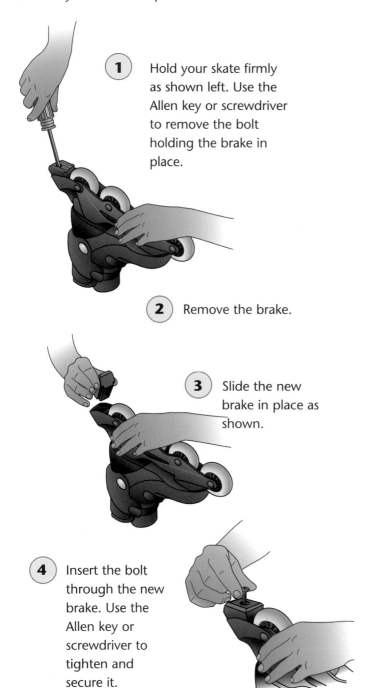

1. Hold your skate firmly as shown left. Use the Allen key or screwdriver to remove the bolt holding the brake in place.

2. Remove the brake.

3. Slide the new brake in place as shown.

4. Insert the bolt through the new brake. Use the Allen key or screwdriver to tighten and secure it.

Your wheels have a "wheelprint" just like your fingerprint. Since every skater skates differently, each skater wears down her wheels in a unique pattern.

Check It Out

R U READY TO ROLL?

Run through this checklist every time you go skating.

✔ Check all the nuts and bolts. Tighten loose ones with an Allen key.

✔ Hold your skate upside down at eye level and look closely at the wheels to check the wear on them.

✔ If your brake is worn down to a wear-limit line or you need to lift your toes more than 45° to stop, replace the brake.

✔ If your skates feel like you're dragging them through mud, it's time to replace the wheels.

Replace the Wheels

Worn out wheels make for a rougher ride.

1. Remove the wheels as shown in "Rotate the Wheels" step 1. Use the bearing popper on the 3-way tool to press on the bearing until it pops out. Do the same on the other bearing.

2. Use a dry cloth to wipe clean the bearings, bearing spacer and inside of the skate frames.

3. Fit together the bearings, bearing spacers and the new wheels (see Wheels, page 25). Follow "Rotate the Wheels" step 3 to screw the new wheels on the frames and adjust them with the Allen keys.

Going Vertical!

Swoosh up, catch air and swoosh back down! For some pro skaters, nothing beats the rush, or thrill, of going vertical—on skates or a skateboard! Check out how they get into the swing of things.

That Swinging Feeling

Believe it or not, skating vert is a lot like swinging in a swing. When you swing, you pump yourself high in the sky. At the top of the swing's path, you stop moving for a split second and feel a moment of weightlessness. Then—*whoosh*—gravity kicks back in and you feel a huge rush as you hurtle back down to Earth.

Pulling Tricks in Thin Air

Vert bladers and skateboarders experience a similar feeling. When they reach the top of a halfpipe ramp, they feel a stall, or moment of weightlessness. And that's when they can launch themselves into the air to do way rad stunts like flips, 720s, grinds, handplants on the coping or fakies (backward moves). Then—*whoosh!*—gravity pulls them back down the ramp to go vertical up the other side!

Pumping to Go Higher

To pull those rad tricks in thin air, vert bladers and skateboarders pump their legs to go higher just like you pump on a swing. As they roll through the flat part of the ramp, they bend their legs to crouch down. Then as they enter the curved, or transition, area, they straighten their legs to stand up. Like coiling and releasing a spring, the work of pumping gives them more energy to go faster. And they need all the speed they can get to ride straight up the vertical and go high in the air.

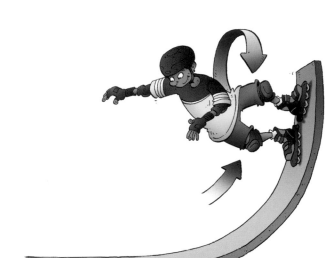

Like a Fly on the Wall

What holds skaters on the vertical so they don't slide down the ramp? (Everybody knows they don't have the sticky wheels—er, feet—of flies…) It's speed and centripetal force—the same force that holds you in a swing as you go vertical. Vert bladers and skateboarders follow a circular path just like you do in a swing. And centripetal force helps them stick to the wall, because it keeps them moving along the circular path. The greater their speed, the stronger the force!

The Vert of Hard Knocks

Doing gravity defying stunts isn't easy. First, vert skaters have to learn how to "pump the ramp"— skate up, turn, and come back down. This takes lots and lots of practice. And it's dangerous stuff. There's just no way to learn it without slamming. In fact, vert bladers and skateboarders have to learn how to fall on the vert, just so they can get back up and fall over and over till they get the moves down. Or is that up? And after they learn how to vault high into the air, they have to master the acrobatic moves of pulling tricks, which leads to more falls. Going vertical sure has its ups and downs!

Fast Fact

Vert inline skating was born when bladers first rolled through a skateboard park full of ramps, halfpipes and empty pools. They got on a roll and kept on going!

Skating Up Mount Kilimanjaro

Everybody thought they were crazy. Many people said they were stupid. And some even laughed in their faces. But that didn't stop Eddy Matzger and Dave Cooper (below) from trying to climb Mount Kilimanjaro, Africa's tallest mountain, in their skates. Why? Well, maybe, because it was there. Just call Mount Kilimanjaro true vertical!

Thick tree roots, grass, boulders, black mud and waist-deep snow covered large parts of the mountain. The pair wore specially designed off-road skates with knobby tires for the 5895 m (19,340 ft) climb in 1998. Since there's no word for skates in Swahili, the locals dubbed their skates "flying shoes." And the name stuck.

When Eddy and Dave tried to "fly" through mud and snow on the mountain, the knobs on their tires gave them better traction than hiking boots! They could duck walk—skate on the toe wheel of one skate and heel wheel of the other—through forest and do crossover steps around boulders. They also used ski-poles to punch the "flying shoes" through deep snow.

Believe it or not, Eddy and Dave made it to the mountaintop (see inset photo). It took them six days to skate up and two to skate back down. And their feet—er, feat—made it into the *Guinness Book of World Records* as "the highest mountain skated." Whew!

Skateboard Wave

Splish, splash! Surfing mania swept across North America like a tidal wave in 1963. Many surfers craved surfing onshore too, so sidewalk surfin'—a.k.a. skateboarding—rolled along in its wake. Pop duo Jan and Dean released a tune called "Sidewalk Surfin'." It climbed up the music charts and fueled the skateboarding fad. Over the next three years, surfers, kids—even ordinary citizens—bought 50 million skateboards.

Hordes of skateboarders barreled along the pavement, using many of the same moves and techniques as surfers. But since skateboards weren't as well made or safe as they are today, the craze soon ground to a stop among all but the most diehard skaters.

With improvements in equipment, skateboarding eventually slid back into favor. Over the last 40 years, this boom–bust–"better it" cycle spun around several times, spawning the boards of today, so that now skateboarding is here to stay. Get the inside scoop on what makes your board skate great.

Skateboard Speak

Hey, thrasher! Are you ready to throw down some phat stuff? Match up these skateboarding terms and their meanings. (Answers on page 64.)

1. fat or phat   **a.** a skateboarder
2. 900   **b.** a jump, using only your feet to bring your skateboard into the air with you
3. ollie   **c.** ramp trick, spinning 2-1/2 times in the air
4. thrasher   **d.** high, far or good

Ollie up and over...

35

The Lean Mean Skateboarding Machine

D on't be fooled by the simple design of a skateboard. This four-wheeled wooden board is a real zoom machine that can launch you into the air for gyrating aerial tricks. Check out the parts that make it zip.

Trucks

Trucks hold the wheels in place. They're made of a metal baseplate attached to the bottom of the deck; a hangar to hold the wheels; a kingpin (or big bolt) through the baseplate and hangar; and urethane cushions called "bushings" that help you steer the board. As you lean, you press down on one side of the bushings, tilting the board and making it go in that direction.

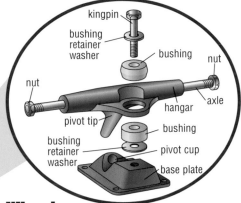

Rail

The edge of the skateboard.

Deck

The deck is the most important part of your skateboard. A top-notch deck is made of Canadian hard rock maple plywood—tough to stand up to everyday riding, and yet flexible to give riders a good feel for the road. The top of the deck is slightly curved up around the edges. This curve helps keep your feet in place, gives you more control and makes the deck stiffer and stronger. Skateboarders stick gritty grip tape on their decks to give their feet better grip for a ripping ride.

Wheels

The type of wheel gives the ride its feel. Soft wheels give you a good grip on the ground and won't get caught on rocks and cracks. Hard wheels give you less grip but more speed. Like inline skates, skateboards have polyurethane wheels and bearings to help them spin smoothly. (See "Clean Your Bearings," page 44)

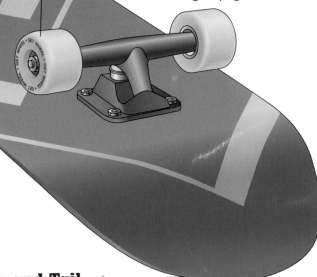

Nose and Tail

The front end of the board is called the nose and the back end the tail. Both ends curve up to help you maneuver the board during tricks. The nose is usually a bit longer and sometimes steeper than the tail. Can you tell which end is which?

Shaped by the Times

Check out some ways the size and shape of skateboards has changed over the years:

1960s

The first manufactured skateboards are shaped like surfboards, with a tapered tail and short nose, to appeal to surfers for "sidewalk surfing."

Early 1970s

Downhill and slalom skateboard riding are all the rage, so skateboards are shaped liked skis. And Tom Sims, who made a "skateboard for the snow," in eighth grade (see page 10), builds a gigantic skateboard out of water skis. It's the world's first longboard—at least, the first on wheels. Huge surfboards called longboards were already being used to cruise the waves.

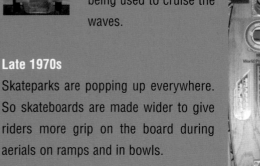

Late 1970s

Skateparks are popping up everywhere. So skateboards are made wider to give riders more grip on the board during aerials on ramps and in bowls.

1990

The year of the Everslick. A skateboard designer puts a wood-bonding plastic on the bottom of a skateboard. The result? More protection for the board, and a skateboard so slippery it slides over almost anything! Everslicks quickly become *the* board to have, but the slick-bottom boards turn out to be just a fad. Within a year, many skaters go back to plain wood boards.

1995

If you ride regularly, eventually you'll trash the deck. It will break, crack or lose its "pop," or strength. Unless the deck is made of NuWood, that is. In 1995, a skateboard company makes the world's first recyclable board out of this high-tech plastic. Instead of throwing out old NuWood boards, skateboarders send them back to the manufacturer to be ground up and recycled.

2003 and Beyond

Skateboards shaped like band-aids are the industry standard. But the root of skateboarding has always been riding your own way. Maybe that's why what's old—longboarding—is suddenly fresh and new again. Longboards give riders more stability and speed. So they can take skaters into terrains like ditches and hills where the only way to ride is to carve out their own lines. As kids forge their own riding styles, they may spur the invention of new techniques and boards to take them where they to want to roll. And so kids on boards will carve out the future of the sport.

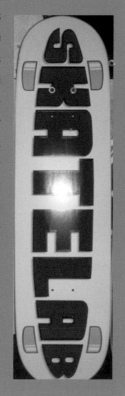

Even pros have a tough time telling the nose from the tail on today's skateboards. In his *Trick Tips* video, Tony Hawk recommends coloring your front bolts to help you tell which end is which. Try it!

All About Balance

Whoa! You can't ride a skateboard without balance. As soon as you step on it, not only does it roll but it also wobbles up and down! Check out the mechanics of getting around on your board.

Finding Balance

How do you balance on a board that wobbles? The key is to spread your weight evenly over the board. Put your front foot over the front bolts and angle it slightly inward. Keep your knees bent. Square your shoulders over your board and put your weight a little forward over your front foot. (If you're leaning too far back, you'll find out when you push. Your board will shoot right out from under you!) Then push with your back foot and keep the foot level with the board as it comes off the ground.

Goofy-Foot? Who, Me?

How can you tell if you're a goofy-footer or a regular rider? While goofy-footers ride with their right foot at the front of the board, regular riders ride with the left foot at the front. It all comes down to which way feels most comfortable for you. To find out, put a skateboard, minus its trucks and wheels, on a carpet and then step back and jump on the board. If your left foot lands at the front, you'll be more comfortable riding regular. But if your right foot lands at the front, goofy is the way to go!

Pushing Forward

You ride a skateboard on your own steam. You propel the board forward by pushing against the ground with your back foot. Pushing gives you momentum. The bigger your stride, the faster you go. But before you can go fast, you need to master balance.

Balancing to Glide

So now you've got momentum and you want to glide. Once you bring your back foot onto the board to glide, you need to reposition your front foot to maintain your balance. Think of your deck as a clock, and turn your front foot to two o'clock (ten if you ride goofy) until your toes hang over the edge. As you turn your foot, turn your shoulders and hips, so they are in line with the board.

Curves Ahead

Believe it or not, that wobble in your board helps you steer. Here's how. Your board wobbles up and down when your weight shifts from one side of the board to the other. As you lean to the right, for example, the right side of your board moves down and the left side moves up. This makes the right wheels bite harder into the ground than the left wheels, which helps the board turn right. So that wobble in your board allows you to turn right or left by simply shifting your weight. Who knew?!

Ollie, Ollie, Up!

How does a skateboard stick to your feet as you whiz through the air? Why doesn't gravity bring it crashing down to the ground? Are skateboarders defying gravity and the laws of physics that rule the world? Well, no (sorry!). But as it turns out, they can use those laws of physics to take them where they want to go. Check out the split-second moves of an ollie and see.

Before the Ollie

As you're gliding with both feet on your skateboard, three forces are acting on your board: your weight, gravity and the force of the ground pushing up against the board. But these forces cancel each other out. So your skateboard zips along at a constant speed.

YOUR WEIGHT

GRAVITY   GROUND

① ②

The Ollie's First Flight

Eyes popped out of their sockets when Alan Gelfand popped the world's first ollie in 1977. No one had ever seen anything like it before. As the 13-year-old skater jumped through the air, his board seemed to magically stick to his feet. In fact, pro skater Stacy Peralta thought it was an illusion. He thought the board was strapped to Alan's feet! The teen skater had invented the trick when he wanted to do something different, and his friends called it the "ollie" after Alan's nickname. Stacy convinced Alan to learn how to pop it off a ramp, and then he brought in photographers so they could unveil the awesome trick to the world. After that, there was no looking back. The ollie completely changed the nature of skateboarding, becoming the basic move of almost every trick on the board!

Crouching Down

When you set up for an ollie, you crouch down slightly. This makes your legs coil up like springs, increasing their potential, or stored energy, so you can jump higher.

Going Up

When your board comes all the way off the ground, your front foot slides forward to the nose of your board. As your foot rubs against the board's rough surface, the force of friction between your foot and the board helps the board stick to your foot. Then your foot can pull the board higher into the air. Now that's phat!

In the Air

Once you're airborne, you push your front foot down and bend your back knee to let the tail of the board come up. This allows the board to level out—and it looks like it's glued to your feet! Once the board is flat and reaches its peak, you straighten both legs a bit. This puts pressure on your board, which helps your feet stick to it as the force of gravity pulls it along with you back down to the ground.

Kicking Down

As you start to ollie, you straighten your legs and raise your arms quickly. Your back foot kicks the tail of your board down. And whether you know it or not, this takes advantage of a universal law of physics: for every action force there is an equal and opposite reaction force. As the tail strikes the ground, the ground pushes up against the tail, propelling your board—and you!—into the air.

Back to Earth

As you land, you bend your knees to absorb some of the shock as the board hits the ground. The ollie has landed!

The Birth of X-treme

Quick! Think fast. When someone says "x-treme sports," what's the first sport that pops into your mind? Skateboarding? If not, think again!

Groundbreaking Wheels

Skateboarding was one of the very first x-treme sports that ever got off the ground. Along with BMX racing, rock climbing and other action sports, it inspired the creation of the X Games.

Almost from the moment the board was invented, skateboarders have wanted to ride to the limit and take it to the max. They've bombed through schoolyards, driveways, lawns, malls, sidewalks, park benches, walls, handrails and even empty swimming pools! In fact, pool riding is where vert skateboarding was born. Nobody knows exactly who that first pool rider was. But we do know that skateboarders were zipping around empty backyard pools as early as 1963.

Pool Riding

Whoever that first pool skater was, it took lots of nerve to drop down the wall and roll foot-first into unknown territory. But skateboarders have always been up for new challenges. And chances are that first pool rider saw nothing but a big smooth concrete bowl—fresh new skating terrain ready to roll on.

After that, it wasn't long before tons of skateboarders were beating their way to empty neighborhood pools. Something had to be done to make pool riding more accessible and safe for skateboarders. But what?

Those empty swimming pools inspired the design of the first skateparks. And, in turn, those first skateparks led to vertical riding in the halfpipe—one of the most popular skateboarding events in the X Games today and the granddaddy of halfpipe inline skating and snowboarding. Some experts say the future of skateboarding lies in park design. They say it won't be the tricks but the terrain they're done on that will define the next wave of skateboarding.

Pushing Limits

Today, skateboard athletes compete in Vert, Street and Best Trick competitions at the X Games. And Games' organizers say the Best Trick competition in skateboarding is pushing all the other sports in the Games to a higher level.

Pro skateboarders are anything but reckless, though. They spend weeks, months and sometimes even years practicing tricks before they get them down. And when it comes to riding walls, rails and ramps, just about any pro would say to go slow and, most importantly, to know when to bail out. Maybe that sounds extreme but—hey— that's skateboarding!

Skatepark Do's and Don't's

While the X Games are for pros, skateparks are for kids. Well-designed skateparks are set up for safe and serious fun. They let you skate at your own level on smooth concrete. They also place runs so you can avoid traffic jams and collisions with other skaters. Here are a few simple do's and don't's for skatepark riding:

- **Do** wear all your safety gear—helmet, knee pads, elbow pads and wrist guards.
- **Do** keep your wits about you. If it gets crowded, be alert so you **don't** collide into other skaters or become an obstacle in another skater's path.
- **Do** skate at your own level. Many parks have areas for beginner, intermediate and expert skaters.
- **Don't** hog a run or ramp when others are waiting to skate it.
- **Do** let every skater have his or her turn.
- **Don't** drop in in front of another skater. Think about it: how would you react if someone snaked you like that?

The Millennium Skatepark in Calgary, Alberta, is the biggest skatepark in the world. With three parks in one— one each for beginner, intermediate and expert skaters—it's larger than a pro football field!

Fast Fact

Ever wondered what it would be like to skate over a taco? Just go to Omaha, Nebraska. A skatepark there includes a cool taco shape with a coping along the edge of the taco. Now that's wacko, er, taco!

Tune Up to Board

If you look after your board, it will look after you. Poor board maintenance is a top cause of skateboarding injuries. Spending a few minutes on maintenance could save you from weeks of no skating because of a needless injury. So break out your tools and let's get down to it!

TOOL BOX

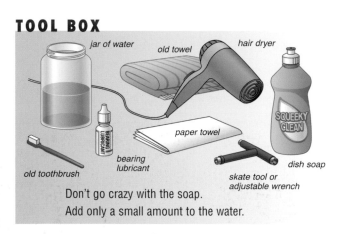

jar of water old towel hair dryer

paper towel

SQUEEKY CLEAN

bearing lubricant

old toothbrush

bearing lubricant

dish soap

skate tool or adjustable wrench

Don't go crazy with the soap. Add only a small amount to the water.

Keep Grip Tape in Shape

Without grip tape, you can forget about pulling tricks, because your feet just won't stay put. Luckily, regular cleaning can help make it last.

1 Clean grip tape with soapy water. Scrub with an old toothbrush or a plastic-bristle brush. But don't soak your board.

2 Dry with an old towel. Let it dry out completely before you ride.

3 To replace worn-out grip tape: loosen the glue by heating with a hair dryer, then peel away as much tape as you can. Stick on new grip tape.

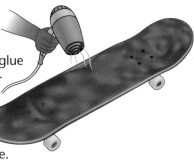

Clean Your Bearings

Need to get your bearings on bearings? They're small parts that sit inside your wheels to help the wheels spin. You need to clean them if you've ridden through dirt or rain, they look black or your ride feels rough. Otherwise, your bearings may rust or break. Not fun!

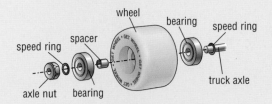

wheel
bearing
speed ring
spacer
speed ring
truck axle
axle nut
bearing

Not all boards have the same set up. Some have speed rings, or washers, and/or a spacer—some don't. Check this pic to make sure you get all your parts back in the right place.

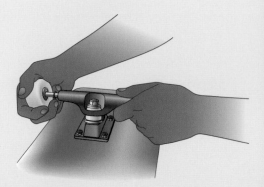

1 Use a skate tool to loosen the axle nut. Slide off the speed ring (if you have one) and the wheel.

2 Put the wheel back on the axle about a quarter of the way. Then use the axle to pop out the bearing as shown. Repeat this on the other side of the wheel to pop out the other bearing. Repeat steps 1 and 2 to remove the other wheels and bearings.

Tune Your Trucks

Does your board feel too wobbly or too hard to turn? You'll need to tune your trucks regularly. As you ride your board, you "work in" the trucks and they become loose. Try adjusting them a few times until your board feels just right.

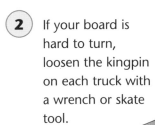
kingpin

1 If your board feels too wobbly, tighten the kingpin on each truck with a skate tool. But don't tighten more than 3 full turns or your bushings may pop and need to be replaced.

2 If your board is hard to turn, loosen the kingpin on each truck with a wrench or skate tool.

Check It Out

R U BOARD READY?

Run through this checklist each time you skate.

✔ Check all the nuts and bolts. If any are loose, tighten them with a wrench or skate tool.

✔ Check your board for cracks or missing chunks. If you find any, have a skate shop replace your deck.

✔ Check wheels for wear, cracks and gouges. If you find any, have a skate shop show you how to replace the wheels.

✔ Check the bushings on your trucks. Have a local shop help you replace any that are cracked or smushed.

✔ If you hear a scraping noise and your board seems to stick and roll unevenly when you ride, your bearings need to be replaced.

Replace Your Bearings

Need to replace worn-out bearings? Do steps 1 to 2 of "Clean Your Bearings." Then do steps 5 and 6 to insert the new bearings.

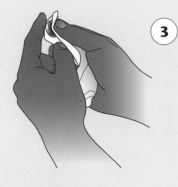

3 Hold a bearing in a paper towel as shown. Then spin the bearing with a finger to clean it. Do the same for each bearing.

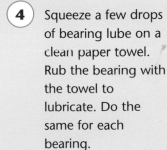

5 Replace the bearings. Put a bearing on a wheel axle. Then put the wheel on the axle and push it over the bearing. Do the same to replace the bearing on the other side of the wheel. Repeat these steps for each wheel.

4 Squeeze a few drops of bearing lube on a clean paper towel. Rub the bearing with the towel to lubricate. Do the same for each bearing.

6 Put the wheel then the speed ring back on the axle. Tighten the axle nut with the skate tool. Do the same for each wheel.

Who Rules the Halfpipe?

W hen it comes to riding the halfpipe and laying down tricks, who rules—skateboarders or snowboarders? Whoever you pick, the fact is that skating the pipe is quite different than snowboarding, or shredding, it, and vice versa. To get the scoop, drop in!

Who Rode It First?

Skateboarders! No doubt about it. They ventured into empty pipes, dams, swimming pools and ditches, looking for a fun ticket to rip. As they rode back and forth, they invented the sport of riding straight up walls and catching big air to pull radical tricks. In fact, when the legendary Terry Kidwell and pals rode the first snowboarding halfpipe, they took moves and tricks from skateboarding and started busting them on their snowboards. Terry believed that snowboarding was more like skateboarding than it was like skiing or surfing. And he went on to almost singlehandedly develop halfpipe shredding.

Who Can Go Higher?

Snowboarders! Top shredders can rocket as high as 4.5 m (15 ft) above the halfpipe's walls on every pass. Since snowboarders' feet are strapped to the board, they don't have to reach down and grab the board to hold it once they're airborne like skateboarders do. (If skateboarders don't grab their board, it will crash back down to Earth. *Wham!*) And this lets snowboarders go higher.

Talkin' Halfpipe

Shredder, Ripper = snowboarder

Bail = throw your board away before you slam

Groovy Graphics Rule

Whether you think skaters or shredders rule the halfpipe, chances are you'd say groovy graphics rule the board. Graphics have no effect on how boards perform, but they can stoke you up to ride. To get punchy graphics on their boards, skateboard and snowboard companies get their team riders to send in ideas. Then graphic designers work the ideas into "board shape," and the riders get together to choose the best ones. Some snowboard companies use kid testers to help design new gear. Once, second-graders in Seattle chose honeycomb-and-bumblebee graphics to give a new board some buzz!

Who Can Bust Bigger Tricks?

Snowboarders! Since shredders can go higher than skaters, they can spend more time up in the air. This extra time allows them to bust bigger tricks. Take aerial spins, for example. While 900s—two-and-a-half full body spins—are rare to pull off in skateboarding, top shredders can bust 1080s (say "ten-eighties")—three full spins in the air.

Who Has to Work Harder?

Skateboarders! Believe it or not, even some snowboarders say skateboarders have to work harder. Here's why. Both riders need speed to ride up the pipe's walls and jump high above the top. So they pump with their legs, crouching down at the bottom of the pipe and then standing up in the curved area. Pumping is hard work and skaters have to pump harder than snowboarders to build up the speed they need.

Who Takes the Bigger Risk?

What's more risky—skateboarding or snowboarding the pipe? It all depends on who you talk to. Some pros say shredding pipe is more risky because your feet are strapped to your board, so you can't jump off and bail when things go wrong. You're stuck on the board and you have to roll with its punches—ow! But others disagree. They say skateboarding requires more physical control, balance and practice. So there's more room for error. What do you think?

Fast Fact

How do you make a halfpipe in the snow? Put Pipe "the magic" Dragon on the job. Once the Pipe Dragon (right) was invented in 1991, the huge snow-grooming machine not only replaced an army of shovels, rakes and people, but it transformed snowy ditches into truly rideable pipes!

900 or Else!

When pro skateboarder Tony Hawk (below) landed the world's first 900 at the Summer X Games in 1999, his first thought was "Finally!" Tony had been dreaming of doing the next-to-impossible trick for 13 years. But that day, it wasn't even on his mind.

Tony was competing in the Best Trick competition for one of the largest crowds skateboarding has ever seen. He was attempting a less difficult version of the trick, the 720 varial—skating up the vertical ramp backward, launching into the air and spinning his body around twice while holding his board with one hand, then turning the board 180 degrees to come down the ramp forward. Halfway into the competition, Tony landed the 720. Whew!

And that's when he decided to go for the 900. He dropped in on the ramp, flew up the other side, spun and—slammed! Then he got up and tried again and again. The announcer said he was out of time, but Tony didn't stop. He kept on trying and, on the twelfth time, Tony landed the trick. After 13 years, Tony finally nailed the 900!

Skateboard Speak

900 = ramp trick in which you spin 2-1/2 times in the air

Snowboard Mode

Get set to rock the halfpipe, ride fakie, bust Canadian Bacon and stomp McTwists. And try not to faceplant as you rip down the slope. Has all that got you stoked, or just confused?

Don't freak! It's just shredder speak. Snowboarders—a.k.a. shredders or rippers—have their own lingo to describe the thrills, spills and chills they experience on the hills. And some of their ripping words come from skateboarding, the same way that many snowboarding moves and tricks come from skateboarding.

Shredders took skateboarding maneuvers to snowy new heights and invented a whole new radical sport. Check out how snowboarding rules the peaks.

Talkin' Shredonics

Snowboarder speak, or "shredonics," is a whole new way to get your point across. Can you match up these ripping words with what they mean? (Answers on page 64.)

1. ripper
2. amped
3. stomp
4. McTwist
5. Canadian Bacon Air

a. a front flip twist with 1-1/2 spins
b. a halfpipe trick: your back hand reaches through your legs to grab your toe edge
c. ready to go
d. snowboarder
e. make a good landing

Slide on over...

Threads to Shred In

Hey, shredders! Here's how to gear up to stay safe and warm on the slopes and still look cool.

Helmet

Don't shred without one. A helmet's strong plastic shell stops things from piercing through and absorbs impacts over a large area to lessen their force. An inner liner crushes up to help absorb the force of an impact. And helmets have vents to let out hot air, so you don't overheat. A hat is no substitute for a helmet. But on cold days, some snowboarders like to wear hats under their helmets for extra warmth.

Goggles

The next time you faceplant, you'll be glad to have your goggles. The tough plastic lenses shield your eyes from snow and harmful UV sun rays. Many goggles have anti-fog lenses, but they still may fog up as your face heats up and sweats.

Binding

See page 52.

Gloves

Get a grip on some waterproof gloves or mitts to keep your hands toasty warm and dry. Snowboarding gloves like these ones come with an outer wrist protector. Broken wrists are the #1 injury in snowboarding. So if your gloves or mitts don't have a wrist protector, use a pair of inline skating or skateboarding wrist guards instead.

Knee and Elbow pads, Butt pad

Just like skateboarders and inline skaters, smart shredders wear knee pads and elbow pads to absorb the force of impact during falls. And those really in the know wear butt pads, too!

Socks

Make sure you wear socks made of wool and nylon or high-tech fabrics that will wick moisture away from your skin to keep your feet dry.

Boots

These boots were made for shredding. Flexible soft boots like these are worn by shredders who like to do halfpipe, freestyle and jumping. Hard boots look like ski boots and are good for racing and exploring mountains. Boots and bindings go together: soft boots with soft bindings, and hard boots with plate bindings. You can't choose one without the other!

When you're buying snowboarding boots, keep in mind that they should be as comfortable to walk in as your sneakers.

Gear Up in Layers

Snowboarders dress in layers so they can easily peel off or add clothes as the outdoor temperature and their body temperature change.

Underwear: The First Layer

Sweat is your body's way of cooling down when it heats up. As sweat evaporates, it cools your skin. But if your skin is wet, you can't stay warm when you're snowboarding. So you won't want to wear cotton longjohns that get soaked in sweat. That's why shredder long underwear is made of fabrics that absorb sweat and wick it away from your skin to keep you dry.

Sweater: The Second Layer

You'll want to wear a sweater or vest made of fleece, pile—a fleecelike fabric—or wool that will let sweat out but keep your body heat in for warmth.

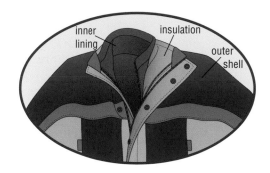

Jacket: The Outer Layer

Your jacket comes between you and the snow. So it's made of tightly woven fabric to protect you from the snow's icy, wet grip. Some jackets have three layers: an inner lining to trap body heat and let sweat out, a thin insulation layer to provide warmth and a waterproof outer shell that lets sweat flow out but stops water and snow from getting in. Other nifty features might include pit vents you can unzip and reinforced elbows for an extra layer of tough fabric right where you need it.

Pants: The Outer Layer

Shredder pants are made of tough waterproof and windproof fabrics. They've also got special features such as high waists to keep out snow. They often have extra padding, made of tough abrasion-resistant fabrics, at the knees and butt—spots that can take a real beating on the hill.

Style—It's in Your Bones

Loose T-shirts, baggy pants, big fleeces, hooded jackets, backward hats…a.k.a shredder style. Snowboarders and skaters wear comfortable, casual clothes that give them lots of room to maneuver as they ollie, rail slide and catch big air on their boards. But some kids wear these clothes without ever hopping on a board—just to look cool! You don't need to spend big bucks or wear certain brands to be a fab skater or snowboarder. You just need to develop your individual style of skating and shredding, and keep practicing to let it get better and better. Yup, style's in your bones, dude!

Rules of the Slopes

- Always gear up in your helmet and protective pads.
- Don't snowboard alone.
- Know your own level. Don't take chances trying tough stunts that are beyond your ability.
- Always stay in control of your snowboard, so you can stop and avoid people or objects that may cross your path.
- Follow the rules of the hill.
- Always give skiers and people ahead of you the right of way. Never cut in front of someone.
- If you want to pass someone, make sure they know you're there. Call out "On your right" or "On your left" so they know which way you're coming.
- Always wear a snowboard leash, so your board doesn't become a dangerous flying object.
- Don't stop on a narrow strip. And if you fall, try to roll out of the way.
- Don't stop where you are invisible to people above you.

Talkin' Shredonics

Faceplant = wipe out and eat snow

Rail = make hard and fast turns

The Lean Mean Shredding Machine

What's the best thing about your board? If you think it's the way it rips, or rides, you're not alone. Check out how the parts of a snowboard help you glide and slide.

Deck

Step right up! The deck is the top of your board where the bindings are mounted and cool graphics rule.

Nose and Tail

On all-mountain and freestyle boards, the nose and tail might look the same. To be sure which is which, turn your board on its side. When the words printed on it are right side up, the nose will be to your left.

Leash

Many places won't let you rip without one. It fastens your front leg to your front binding. That way if your board starts to go astray, it can't fly far away and bonk people all the way down the hill.

Edges

Edges give you an "edge." These thin strips of steel run from nose to tail to help you grip the snow. The toeside edge is closest to your toes, while the heelside edge is closest to your heels.

Sidecut

Your board has a narrow waist. As it flexes during a turn, this sidecut contacts the slope and helps you carve, or sink your edge into the snow. The deeper the sidecut, the sharper and smaller your turns.

Bindings

Bindings fasten your boots to your board. Most snowboard bindings don't release if you fall. They're designed to make you and your board one lean mean shredding machine.

Stomp pad

This rubber or plastic mat holds your back foot on the board when it's not strapped into the binding. Without it, your foot could slip off the board, hit the ground, and pull your legs apart.

Base

The base is the bottom of your board that slides on the snow. It's made of polyethylene—the same plastic that grocery bags are made of!

Snowboards come in three basic types: freestyle for trick riding, freeriding for all-terrain riding, and alpine carving/racing for high-speed riding.

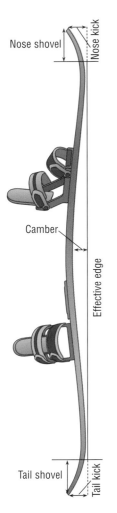

Nose shovel

Nose kick

Camber

Effective edge

Tail shovel

Tail kick

Nose and Tail shovels

Does your board shovel snow? Well, no. Its scoop-shaped shovels, or kicks, help it float to the top of the snow. A high nose kick helps you clear obstacles; a low one has less drag. On most freestyle boards, the nose kick and tail kick are virtually the same, so it's easy to ride forward or fakie.

Effective edge

Also called the running length, this is the length of your board that contacts the snow when you're standing on your board. The longer your board's effective edge, the more grip you have on the snow and the more stable you are.

Camber

The camber, or arch, transmits the force of your weight along the whole edge of the board. When you stand on your board, it flexes and flattens out. This gives your board a better grip on the snow when you turn and carve. The camber also works like a spring, pushing your board from one turn to the next. It makes your board fun to ride!

Snowboard Sandwich, Anyone?

Your board is like a multi-decker sandwich! Though the exact recipe is a carefully guarded secret, we do know this much: board "chefs" make snowboard "sandwiches" from the inside out. They start with a flexible wood or polyurethane core that gives the board its feel when you ride it. Next, they carefully layer on fiberglass, rubber, graphite and Kevlar for strength. If the mix is too flexible, they might end up with a "noodle"—a board that buckles; if it's too stiff, a "cracker"—a board that breaks. Board chefs top it off with a sheet of plastic, graphics and clear lacquer finish for greater scratch resistance. They also add a base of strong, smooth plastic, called P-Tex™, which holds wax and helps the board glide. Chomp, er, stomp that.

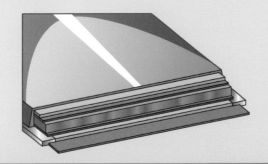

Tips for Choosing a Board

- If you're looking for your first board, go for a freeriding or all-mountain board designed for all terrains and conditions. Ask for a board with lots of flex rather than stiffness, because it will be easier to maneuver.
- Use your weight, height and foot size as a buying guide:

29 to 47 kg (65–105 lbs)	125 to 135 cm (49–53 in) long
45 to 70 kg (100–150 lbs)	140 to 160 cm (55–63 in) long
70 kg (150 lbs)	150 to 170 cm (59–67 in) long

Then stand the board on the ground to see if it reaches between your chin and nose. And make sure it's wide enough so your feet don't hang over the edge when you're strapped into the bindings.
- Resist the temptation to buy a board for its cool graphics.
- Don't buy your favorite (or any other) pro's model without test riding it first. Pro models are designed for a particular rider's height and weight and how he or she likes to shred. If your body stats aren't the same and you like shredding differently, chances are the board won't perform as well beneath your own two feet.

Talkin' Shredonics

Fakie = backward, or tail first

The Downhill Shred

Hey, shred head! You're at the top of the mountain and you're ready to go. Check out the mechanics of ripping down the slope—and look out below!

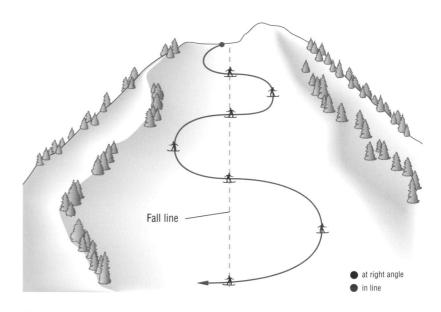

The more you ride in line (parallel) to the fall line, the faster you'll go. On the other hand, the more you ride at right angles (perpendicular) to the fall line, the slower you'll go. And if you're at a full right angle to it, you'll come to a full stop.

Gravity Rules

What makes snowboarding completely different from skateboarding, scootering or blading—besides the snow? Gravity. You don't have to push your snowboard down a mountain the way you push a skateboard, inline skates or a scooter along the ground. Gravity, the natural force that attracts things to the Earth, pulls it down—whether you're ready or not. *Whooosh!*

Down the Fall Line

Say you checked that the slope above was clear and you dropped a snowball—or even your snowboard!—down. Gravity would yank it down the fall line— an imaginary line along the steepest path from the top to the bottom of the slope. It's the most direct route down the mountain. So it's usually not a straight line— it often zigzags down the mountain as the direction of the slope changes.

Fall Line = Fast Lane

But what has the fall line got to do with you shredding down a mountain? Lots! It's the path gravity pulls you down. As you start sliding down a slope, your board follows the fall line and picks up speed, or accelerates. And the longer you're in the fall line, the faster you go. So shredders make turns across the fall line to slow down, so they can control their speed. That's why it's a good idea to look for the fall line and plan where to make your turns before you let 'er rip.

Board Under Pressure

Don't have a conniption if you find yourself speeding out of control as you turn across the fall line. Just try bending your knees more to push down on the uphill edge of your board. Sinking into the turn like this will help control your speed. And that's a good thing. Since the base of your board is made of smooth plastic that slides easily on slippery ice and snow, you need all the control you can get!

Talkin' Shredonics

Bust = to do

Stoked = thrilled

Carve or Starve!

Carve down the mountain or stay at the top and starve! That seems to be the motto of many expert shredders and racers. For many, carving, or slicing one edge of the board and then the other into the snow, is the only way to go. Riding on the edges like this gives them more control over their speed and direction than riding on a flat board. The edges grip the snow, so the rider is less likely to be knocked about or thrown off course if the board hits a rut or bump. Carving also gives racers more speed, because they don't skid as they turn.

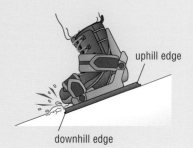

Shredding's Golden Rule

Always control your snowboard with the uphill edge—never the downhill edge. Why? What happens if you dig your downhill edge into the snow? *Kerplop!* Your board jerks forward, hurling you into the snow face-first or onto the back of your head. Ouch!

uphill edge

downhill edge

Fall Line Jitters

Even pros can get the willies about riding straight down the fall line. In one giant slalom snowboard race in 2000, champion rider Chris Klug thought the course had been set too straight down the fall line. The mountain was icy and he thought he'd pick up too much speed to control. But once he ran the course, he realized it was actually quite "turny," and he won the race!

No Kidding, We're Jibbing

Tree: dead ahead. Handrail: coming up on the left. No problem, if you're an experienced jibber, that is. Trees, handrails, picnic tables, mailboxes and cars aren't in the way for pro jibbers. They're rideable terrain. Jibbers bonk, or hit, trees with their boards and jib, or slide, their boards across rails, logs and cars. Jibbing is a type of snowboarding that's a lot like street skateboarding. It got going in the early 1990s when a couple of riders were looking to throw down new tricks, and today many snowboard parks are built with rails, stairs and other rideable objects. At the 2001 JibFest in Big Bear, California, riders got stoked jibbing the Curve-a-tron, a curved rail built into a bank, and the Monster S, a 12-m (40-ft) long S-shaped rail. Riders everywhere want dibs on the jib!

Shredders Storm the Olympics

Competing at the Olympics is *the* athletic dream. Rippers got the chance in 1998, when snowboarding became an Olympic sport. Here's the scoop on the two snowboarding events included in the Games.

Parallel Giant Slalom

On your mark, get set, shred! There's not a moment to lose as two snowboarders go head to head, busting a 3000-m (9843-ft) course. They rip down the course at about 80 km/h (50 mph), railing around 30 to 50 triangular gates.

Racing the course is no easy job. Skid around a gate and you'll lose precious seconds. Miss one gate and you're disqualified. Speed out of control and you'll crash. Whoa! Luckily, competitors have a chance to check out the course, gates and condition of the snow before the race. Then they can plan their run and go for gold.

Halfpipe

It's totally gnarly. It's full of sick tricks. It's an Olympic competition like no other: the halfpipe snowboard event! Where else can you find athletes competing with glitter in mohawk-spiked hair or listening to their own tunes on headphones as they compete? The fact is, halfpipe rippers ride to their own rhythm.

It takes individual style, nerves of steel and rock-solid tricks to compete in the halfpipe. Snowboarders drop down a snowy chute, or U-shaped course, and ride up and down the walls. To gain speed, they carve across the bottom of the course or pump up the walls. Then they launch themselves into the air to try to pull difficult tricks with perfect form.

Shredders catch big air, some soaring 4.5 m (15 ft) above the top of the wall. Then they pull McTwists, rodeo flips (partly inverted 360s with a backflip), stale fish (using the back hand to grab the heel edge behind the back leg between the bindings) or stiffys (jumps with both legs straight). And every snowboarding season they invent new moves to throw into the mix.

The competitors bust six to eight maneuvers while a panel of judges score them out of 10, awarding points for basic maneuvers, height, landing, technical difficulty and overall impression. The competitor with the highest score wins!

Whatever the Weather

Competitors have to adjust to changing conditions on the fly. Check out some of the different types of snow they slide on.

"DEATH COOKIES" That's what one competitor called the chunks of ice on the course at the 1998 Olympics in Nagano, Japan. The mixture of newly fallen snow, hard-packed snow and ice made the course difficult to ride without wiping out.

POWDER Powder is light, dry snow that riders adore. The key to riding in it is to keep the nose of your board above the snow and ride with enough speed so you don't sink. Since powder is soft, it's the best snow to land tricks on—not to mention to fall on.

MASHED POTATOES Heavy, wet snow can bog you down. Even though mashed potatoes are practically the opposite of powder, you ride them the same way.

CORN SNOW Corn snow is powder that has thawed and then refrozen into small chunks like kernels of corn. It makes it easy for shredders to control their speed, and some like it just as much powder.

Olympic "No Gos"

Not all shredders were stoked when snowboarding became an Olympic event. Some flat-out refused to go. They felt like it would be selling out—competing for fame and the chance to earn big bucks rather than for the joy of snowboarding itself. And it didn't help that the Olympics put skiers in charge of the sport. The way the judges rated the routines meant that some rockin' rippers pulled back on their jaw-dropping moves to score points. What's more, for many snowboarders, what they do is about more than competing. It's about riding the mountain their own way to express themselves. Go, dudes!

Tune Up to Shred

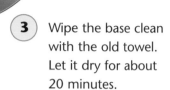

Want to get your thrills on the hill? Try waxing your board every three times you shred. Or, if you're really keen to slide, wax every time you ride! Wax cuts down drag, to maximize your glide. It also protects your board.

③ Wipe the base clean with the old towel. Let it dry for about 20 minutes.

Wax to Slide

① Cover the floor of your work area with old newspapers. Set up your board on old phone books, wooden blocks or a work bench as shown below.

② To get the most out of your wax job, you need to clean away dirt, grime and excess wax first. Put on your rubber gloves. Give the base 4 squirts of citrus cleaner and let it sink in for a few minutes.

Tail

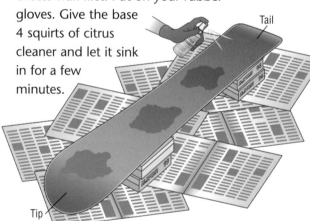

Tip

④ Turn on the iron to medium heat. Let it warm so it's hot enough to melt the wax. Hold the iron above your board. Touch the wax to the iron and drip the melting wax onto your board as shown. If the wax smokes, the iron's too hot—turn it down.

TOOL BOX

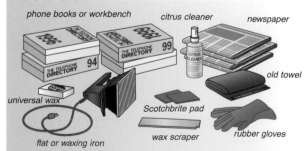

phone books or workbench — citrus cleaner — newspaper

old towel

universal wax

flat or waxing iron — wax scraper — rubber gloves — Scotchbrite pad

Safety Alert: Wax your board in a well-ventilated area. Do not use a household iron: use a flat or ski iron that has no holes in the base. Ask an adult to help you with the iron.

The Happy Boarder Kit

Put this stuff in your bag, dude. Then you'll be prepared to make the most out of every day on the hill.

✔ Water pack (As the pros say, "Hydrate or die!")
✔ Extra mitts, socks, goggles (If you don't need 'em, a friend might.)
✔ All-in-one tool (If need be, you can tighten your bindings on the spot.)
✔ Extra nuts and bolts (If they fall off, what are the chances of finding them in the snow?)
✔ Extra boot lace (You just never know when one might go…)
✔ Lock (Having your board stolen sucks!)

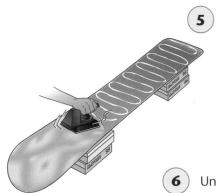

5 Iron the wax from tip to tail to cover the whole base evenly. KEEP THE IRON MOVING or else you may burn your board!

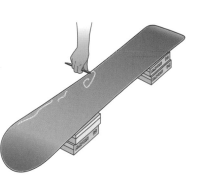

6 Unplug the iron. Let the wax sink into the pores of your board and cool for 10 to 15 minutes. Scrape off the excess wax. Pulling the scraper toward you (if you push, it might slip and hurt you), swipe the scraper from tip to tail in one direction a few times until no more wax comes off.

7 Remove excess wax from your edges. Fit the scraper's nick onto the edge, then swipe it from tip to tail.

8 Buff, or texture, the base. Rub a Scotchbrite™ pad from tip to tail a few times as shown. This will help create channels for water to flow off your board as you ride.

Only the base and edges of your board touch the snow. So if you keep the base well waxed, you're bound to have a fast ride with good glide.

Check It Out

R U SHRED READY?

OK. Faceplants and wipeouts are facts of life on the hill. But nobody wants to fall any more than absolutely necessary—especially due to equipment glitches. So run through this checklist before you hit the slopes. Then you can fix any trouble before it makes you eat snow!

✔ Check your bindings. Are the straps in good condition? If not, have them repaired or replaced before you go shredding.

✔ Are your bindings firmly bolted to your board? They should feel stiff not loose. Check all the nuts and bolts and tighten any that are loose.

✔ Check that your leash is securely fastened to the key ring on your boot.

✔ Is your stomp pad securely in place? If not, adjust it.

AFTER RIDE CARE

Once you call it quits for the day, check your board to keep it in tip-top riding condition:

✔ Wipe your board and bindings dry with a clean towel.

✔ Make sure you dry the edges to help prevent them from rusting out.

✔ Check the base of your board for dings or gouges, and have them repaired by your local snowboard shop before you hit the slopes again. If snow gets into your board, it will rot from the inside out!

✔ Are there any dry spots on the base? If so, it needs to be waxed.

✔ Gently run a fingernail over your edges to check if they're still sharp. If not, have them sharpened at a local snowboard shop.

The Ultimate Board Grrl

Just call Carolyn Kunkel an all-around board grrl. She started skateboarding for the challenge of it when she was nine. And today, not only is she a pro snowboarder, but she surfs, skateboards and even mountain boards. Carolyn says the moves of one board sport transfer to the next. "Sometimes when I'm surfing, I'll be doing something from snowboarding," and vice versa.

Her friends call her C-Roll, her name minus the *a*, because she's always on the roll! From November to April, she's practically glued to her snowboard, shredding down the slopes of Colorado. And in the summer, she hits the trails on her mountain board—a board built with offroad tires and a suspension system to ride mountains when there's no snow. In fact, Carolyn is the first woman in the world to ever ride a mountain board. That first ride was fun and pretty much got her hooked, she says.

In 1997, she took two mountain boards to Mount Verbier, Switzerland, where she was coaching a snowboard summer camp. And that's when she became the first person to mountain board down the 3300 m (10,872 ft) mountain, cruising past wildflowers, grass and cows. When it comes to a fun challenge, Carolyn's first in line on her board!

Pro rider Carolyn Kunkel loves to mountain board in Colorado, where she can take her board on chairlifts and rip on down (top). Check out Carolyn catching huge air in Long Island, New York—becoming the only woman in the world to drop down this 10-m (35-foot) ramp on a mountain board and stick it clean (bottom).

Catch Phat Air Everywhere!

Want a stick you can ride absolutely anywhere? Hop on an all-terrain board—a.k.a. mountain board or dirt board—and rip hard carves on grass, dirt, rocks or concrete. ATBs sport big air-filled tires, shock absorbers and bindings for your feet. That way you can bounce over almost anything—logs, bumps and jumps—*boing*! They also have decks that tilt more than skateboards so you can carve bigger turns. And some even have brakes. Snowboarders invented ATBs in their garages in the 1970s so they could ride when there was no snow. And this just may be what makes all-terrain boarding a fast-growing sport all over the world. Since you don't need snow or a mountain to ride, you've got no limits. You can go huge anytime, anywhere.

BOARDER BIO

Name: Carolyn Kunkel

Age: 27

Home: Long Island, New York

Nickname: C-Roll

#1 Board Trick: Backside 360 grab

Favorite Sport: Snowboarding

On Being Airborne: It feels like flying.

#1 Tip for Kids: Wear safety gear—a helmet, wrist guards, knee pads and a butt pad.

# of Tries to Learn a New Move: It depends on the move, but usually it takes me 10 to 20 tries.

Difference between snowboarding and mountain boarding: A mountain board is heavier, so you need more momentum.

Wildest Mountain board Ride: Just recently there was a big air contest, where I went down a 10-m (35-foot) drop-in ramp and then over a 6-m (20-foot) gap (see left). It was pretty wild! I was the first woman to do it on a mountain board.

Glossary

720 a ramp trick in which pros complete two full-body spins in the air

900 a ramp trick in which pros complete two-and-a-half full-body spins in the air

1080 a ramp trick in which pros complete three full-body spins in the air

adjustable wrench tool for loosening and tightening nuts and bolts of different sizes

aggressive skating stunt skating on ramps and rails; see *X-treme*

all-in-one tool a tool for adjusting snowboard bindings, nuts, and bolts

all-terrain board, also *mountain board* or *dirtboard* a board with off-road tires and suspension that's built to ride anywhere

Allen key an L-shaped tool designed to fit into and turn a hexagonal screw or bolt

ankle cuff the part of an inline skate that gives the ankle extra support

ankle strap a strap around the ankle of an inline skate designed to give the ankle extra support

axle a shaft, or rod, that holds wheels

baseplate the metal part that attaches a truck to the bottom of a skateboard deck

bearings tiny balls inside a metal shield in wheels that help the wheels turn smoothly

bindings clamps that fasten your boots to your snowboard

blades a pair of inline skates

blading inline skating

bolt a metal rod with a head used for holding parts together

boot part of an inline skate that holds your foot; footwear for snowboarding

brake a pad at the back of an inline skate used for stopping; a rear wheel guard on the back wheel of a scooter, or a hand lever, used for stopping

bunkering sliding down a snowy hill on a sled made from barrel slats

bushings urethane cushions in a skateboard truck

camber the arch of the bottom of a snowboard

carve to slice a snowboard's edges into the snow

centripetal force a force that acts on an object to keep it in circular motion

coping the rail at the top of a ramp

core or hub the center of an inline wheel that holds the bearings in place

corn snow *powder* that has thawed and then refrozen into small chunks like corn kernels

crate a box or case made of slatted wood

deck the footboard of a scooter, skateboard, or snowboard

durometer the measure of a wheel's hardness

edge the thin steel strip along the side of a snowboard that helps grip the snow

effective edge the length of a snowboard that contacts the snow

fall line an imaginary line that's the most direct route down a mountain

fork the part of a scooter frame that holds the front wheel

frame the part of an inline skate that holds the wheels on the bottom of the boot

giant slalom a downhill snowboarding event on a long zigzag course with wide turns

goofy-foot riding a skateboard or snowboard with the right foot at the front of the board instead of the left foot

gravity a natural force that attracts objects to the Earth

grease a thick oily lubricant

grip tape gritty, bumpy tape that sticks to scooter and skateboard decks to give riders' feet grip

halfpipe a U-shaped ramp that has vertical walls that go straight up and down

handbrake a lever mounted on a scooter's handlebars that's used to bring the scooter to a stop

handlebars the bars you hold to steer a scooter

hangar the part of a skateboard truck that holds the wheels in place

inline skates skates for dry land with wheels attached to the soles in a straight line

jibbing riding a snowboard on rails, logs, cars and other obstacles

kingpin a big bolt in a skateboard truck through the baseplate and the hangar

leash a short cord that fastens your front leg to the front binding on your snowboard so your snowboard can't fly away from you

liner the padding inside the boot of an inline skate

longboard a skateboard 90 cm (36 inches) or more in length, named after longer-than-average surfboards

mashed potatoes what snowboarders call heavy, wet snow

momentum the force or energy of a moving body

motor scooter a scooter powered by an onboard motor

nose the front end of a skateboard or snowboard

nut a small piece of metal with a threaded hole in it that's used to secure a bolt

parallel giant slalom a snowboard race in which two riders ride down a long mountain course to try to reach the finish line first

polyurethane the material that inline skate, scooter, and skateboard wheels are made of; see *urethane*

pool riding riding a skateboard in an empty pool

powder what snowboarders call light dry snow

profile the shape of a wheel

pump to build up speed with your legs by crouching down at the bottom of a halfpipe then standing up in the curved area

push scooter a scooter that you ride on your own power by pushing your foot against the ground

quarterpipe a halfpipe with only one wall

rail the edge of a skateboard

rear wheel guard the metal cover on a scooter's back wheel that shields you from mud and water and may act as a brake

reflector an object that reflects light to make whatever it's attached to more visible

right of way the right of one rider, or skater, to proceed before another

roller skates skates with wheels attached to the soles at the front and back

sidecut the narrow waist of a snowboard that helps you carve

skatepark a park designed for inline skating or skateboarding

skate tool a tool for adjusting screws and nuts on a skateboard

spacer a metal part that keeps the bearing shields inside a wheel from touching each other

speed ring a washer in a skateboard wheel that prevents the bearings from rubbing the axle nut or truck, so they can spin freely

stall the moment of weightlessness when vert skaters can launch themselves into the air to perform tricks

steer tube the part of a scooter's frame that turns the wheels in the same direction as you turn the handlebars

steer tube clamp the lever that adjusts the height of the handlebars on a scooter

stomp pad a rubber or plastic mat, or disks, on your snowboard that hold your back foot on the board when it's not in the binding

surfing riding ocean waves standing on a surfboard

suspension system shock absorbers that look like coiled springs and help make the ride feel smooth

tail the back end of a skateboard or snowboard

terrain ground, or area, characterized by certain natural features

three-way (or 3-way) tool a tool with three heads—screwdriver, Allen key and bearing popper—for adjusting inline skates

truck the metal part of a skateboard attached to the bottom of the deck that holds the wheels in place

T-tube the part of a scooter that holds the handlebars in place

urethane what skateboarders call polyurethane; see *polyurethane*

wheel a circular object that helps vehicles and skates roll over the ground

X Games a mini-Olympics for extreme sports

X-treme or extreme aggressive stunt moves on scooters, inline skates, skateboards or snowboards; these action sports also include BMX racing, bungee jumping and rock climbing

INDEX

A
aggressive skates, 29
aggressive skating, 12, 27, 28–29
all-in-one tool, 58
all-terrain board (ATB), 52, 53, 60, 61
Allen key, 18, 30

B
Bahne, Bob, 10
balance, 15, 38–39
bearings, 25, 31, 44–45
Big Bear, CA, 55
bindings, 52, 59
blades, 11, 23–34 See also inline skates and
   roller skates
   gear, 6
   off-road skates, 34
   parts, 24–25
   tricks, 26, 28–29, 32–33
   tune-up, 30–31
   x-treme scene, 28–29, 32–33
Blank, Brad "Squeak," 9
BMX biking, 17, 42
boot, 24, 50
brake, 14, 15, 24, 31
Brazil, 29
Britain, 7
Brunswick Sporting Goods Company, 10
bungee jumping, 12
bunkering, 9
Burton Snowboards, 11

C
California, 5, 9, 10, 11
camber, 53
Carpenter, Jake Burton, 11
carve, 55
centripetal force, 33
Chicago Roller Skate Company, 10
Children's Museum of Manhattan, 20
Colorado, 60
Cook, James, 8
Cooper, Dave, 34

D
DaSilva, Fabiola, 29
dirt board See all-terrain board

E
effective edge, 53
elbow pads See protective pads
Everslick, 37

F
Fabiola Rule, 29
fall line, 54, 55
Flying Squirrel, 13, 17
friction, 41
Friedkin, Lee, 15

G
gear, 5, 6, 43, 50–51
Gelfand, Alan, 40
giant slalom, 12
goggles, 50
goofy-foot, 39
gravity, 32, 33, 40, 54
grip tape, 44
Grismer, Lisa, 17
Gropaiz, Fabrice, 25
Guinness Book of World Records, 17, 34

H
halfpipe, 46–47, 57
Hawaii, 8
Hawk, Tony, 17, 37, 39, 48
helmet, 5, 6, 50, 61

I
ice skates, 7, 12
inline skates, 8, 10, 12 See also blades

J
J.D. Corporation, 12
jibbing, 55
jumping, 26, 32–33

K
Kidwell, Terry, 46
Klug, Chris, 55
knee pads See protective pads
Kunkel, Carolyn, 60–61

L
Lausanne, Switzerland, 28
leash, 52, 59
Lewis, Daphne, 16
LIFE magazine, 10
Lightning™ skate, 11
lingo, 5, 7, 8, 13, 17, 23, 26, 29, 35, 46,
   48, 49, 51, 53, 54
Long Island, NY, 60, 61
longboard See skateboards

M
Makaha (skateboard company), 9
Matzger, Eddy, 34
McGee, Pat, 10
Merlin, Joseph, 7
Millennium Skatepark, Calgary, AB, 43
Milovich, Dimitrije, 11
momentum, 39, 61
motor scooter, 9
Mount Kilimanjaro, Africa, 34
Mount Verbier, Switzerland, 60
mountain board See all-terrain board

N
Nagano, Japan, 12, 56, 57
Nasworthy, Frank, 10
Netherlands, 7
New Jersey, 10

O
ollie, 40–41
Olson, Brennan and Scott, 11
Olympics, 12, 56–57
Omaha, NE, 43

P
parallel giant slalom, 56
Peralta, Stacy, 40
Petitbled, Monsieur, 8
Pier Avenue Junior High, Hermosa, CA, 9
Poppen, Sherman and Wendy, 10
protective pads, 5, 6, 50, 61

Q
quarterpipe, 17

R
Razor™ Scooter, 12
Razor Rage National Scooter Series, 17
Reid, Jarret, 17
Reid, Wyatt, 17
rock climbing, 42
roller skates, 7, 8, 10, 20 See also blades
Rollerblades™, 11
Ruby (the rottweiler), 16

S
safety, 5, 6, 43, 44, 50–51, 61
Scandinavia, 7
scooters, 13–22
   gear, 6
   parts, 14
   tricks, 17
   tune-up, 18–19
   x-treme scene, 16–17
Seattle, WA, 16
Shear, Alex, 20–21
Sims, Tom, 10, 37
Sims Snowboards, 10
skate tool, 44
skateboards, 10, 12, 32–33, 35–48, 60
   balance to ride, 38–39
   first manufactured, 9
   gear, 6
   longboard, 37
   ollie, 40–41
   parts, 36
   pool riding, 42
   tricks, 46–47
   tune-up, 44–45
   x-treme scene, 32–33, 42–43
skateparks, 5, 11, 28, 29, 37, 42, 43
Sked (or Rocket Ski), 21
Sno-Scooter, 15
snow conditions, 57
snowboards, 10, 49–61
   first manufactured, 11
   gear, 50–51
   Olympics, 12, 56–57
   parts, 52–53
   recognition as official sport, 11
   tips for choosing a board, 53
   tricks, 46–47, 57
   tune-up, 58–59
   types of, 52, 53
   x-treme scene, 56–57
Snurfer, 10, 11
Solar Scooter, 22
SoloTrek XFV, 22
stunts See tricks
surfing, 8, 9, 11, 35, 60

T
three-way (3-way) tool, 30
tricks, 17, 26, 28–29, 32–33, 40–41, 42–43,
   46–47, 48, 57
Trikke™, 12
Tsai, Gino, 12
Tyers, Robert John, 8

U
United Specialities Company, 9

V
Ventura, CA, 11
Volito, 8

W
water ski, 9, 37
Wee Wheeler, 9
wheels, 7, 10, 11, 14, 19, 25, 31, 36
Winterstick, 11
wrist guards, 6, 50, 61

X
X Games, 12, 29, 42, 48

Answers
Words to Skate By (page 23): 1. d, 2. c, 3.
a, 4. e, 5. f, 6. b; Skateboard Speak (page
35): 1. d, 2. c, 3. b, 4. a; Talkin' Shredonics
(page 49): 1. d, 2. c, 3. e, 4. a, 5. b